Elements of Literature®
Fourth Course

Vocabulary Development
with Answer Key

- **Vocabulary Development Worksheets**
- **Cumulative Vocabulary Reviews**

HOLT, RINEHART AND WINSTON
A Harcourt Education Company

Orlando • **Austin** • New York • San Diego • Toronto • London

Copyright © by Holt, Rinehart and Winston

All rights reserved. No part of this publication may be reproduced or transmitted in any form or by any means, electronic or mechanical, including photocopy, recording, or any information storage and retrieval system, without permission in writing from the publisher.

Teachers using ELEMENTS OF LITERATURE may photocopy blackline masters in complete pages in sufficient quantities for classroom use only and not for resale.

ELEMENTS OF LITERATURE, HOLT, and the "Owl Design" are trademarks licensed to Holt, Rinehart and Winston, registered in the United States of America and/or other jurisdictions.

Printed in the United States of America

> If you have received these materials as examination copies free of charge, Holt, Rinehart and Winston retains title to the materials and they may not be resold. Resale of examination copies is strictly prohibited.

> Possession of this publication in print format does not entitle users to convert this publication, or any portion of it, into electronic format.

TABLE OF CONTENTS

To the Teacher vii
How to Use a Dictionary viii
Pronunciation and Spelling Guide ix

COLLECTION 1
PLOT AND SETTING • SYNTHESIZING SOURCES

Contents of the Dead Man's Pocket • *Jack Finney* 1

Double Daddy • *Penny Parker*
Diary of a Mad Blender • *Sue Shellenbarger*
The Child's View of Working Parents • *Cora Daniels* 2

The Leap • *Louise Erdrich* 3

The Pedestrian • *Ray Bradbury* 4

Cumulative Vocabulary Review, Collection 1 5

COLLECTION 2
CHARACTER • USING PRIMARY AND SECONDARY SOURCES

Everyday Use • *Alice Walker* 7

Two Kinds • *Amy Tan* 8

By Any Other Name • *Santha Rama Rau* 9

Cumulative Vocabulary Review, Collections 1–2 10

COLLECTION 3
NARRATOR AND VOICE • GENERATING RESEARCH QUESTIONS

The Storyteller • *Saki* 12

The Cold Equations • *Tom Godwin* 13

Taste—The Final Frontier • *Esther Addley* 15

Typhoid Fever *from* **Angela's Ashes** • *Frank McCourt* 16

Cumulative Vocabulary Review, Collections 1–3 17

Vocabulary Development **iii**

COLLECTION 4
COMPARING THEMES • EVALUATING ARGUMENTS: PRO AND CON

Catch the Moon • *Judith Ortiz Cofer* 19

The Bass, the River, and Sheila Mant • *W. D. Wetherell* 20

And of Clay Are We Created • *Isabel Allende* 21

The Man in the Water • *Roger Rosenblatt* 22

If Decency Doesn't, Law Should Make Us Samaritans •
   Gloria Allred and *Lisa Bloom*
Good Samaritans U.S.A. Are Afraid to Act • *Ann Sjoerdsma* 23

Cumulative Vocabulary Review, Collections 1–4 24

COLLECTION 5
IRONY AND AMBIGUITY • GENERATING RESEARCH QUESTIONS AND EVALUATING SOURCES

Lamb to the Slaughter • *Roald Dahl* 26

R.M.S. Titanic • *Hanson W. Baldwin* 27

from **Into Thin Air** • *Jon Krakauer* 28

Explorers Say There's Still Lots to Look For •
   Helen O'Neill 29

Notes from a Bottle • *James Stevenson* 30

Cumulative Vocabulary Review, Collections 1–5 31

COLLECTION 6
SYMBOLISM AND ALLEGORY • SYNTHESIZING SOURCES

Through the Tunnel • *Doris Lessing* 33

Coming of Age, Latino Style: Special Rite Ushers Girls into Adulthood • *Cindy Rodriguez*
Vision Quest • *from* Encyclopaedia Britannica
Crossing a Threshold to Adulthood • *Jessica Barnes* 34

The Masque of the Red Death • *Edgar Allan Poe* 35

Cumulative Vocabulary Review, Collections 1–6 36

COLLECTION 8
EVALUATING STYLE • EVALUATING AN ARGUMENT

Night Calls • *Lisa Fugard* 38

Call of the Wild—Save Us! • *Norman Myers* 39

A Very Old Man with Enormous Wings •
  Gabriel García Márquez 40

Cumulative Vocabulary Review, Collections 1–8 41

COLLECTION 9
BIOGRAPHICAL AND HISTORICAL APPROACH • USING PRIMARY AND SECONDARY SOURCES

Where Have You Gone, Charming Billy? • *Tim O'Brien* 43

The War Escalates *from* The American Nation • *Paul Boyer*
Dear Folks • *Kenneth W. Bagby*
from **Declaration of Independence from the War in Vietnam** •
  Martin Luther King, Jr. 44

The Sword in the Stone *from* Le Morte d'Arthur •
  Sir Thomas Malory, retold by *Keith Baines* 45

The Tale of Sir Launcelot du Lake *from* Le Morte d'Arthur •
  Sir Thomas Malory, retold by *Keith Baines* 46

Cumulative Vocabulary Review, Collections 1–9 47

Vocabulary Development **V**

COLLECTION 10
DRAMA • EVALUATING AN ARGUMENT

The Brute • *Anton Chekhov* 49

***Julius Caesar* in an Absorbing Production •**
  John Mason Brown 50

Cumulative Vocabulary Review, Collections 1–10 51

ANSWER KEY 53

To the Teacher

Vocabulary Development

The *Vocabulary Development* copying masters are one- or two-page worksheets that expand on students' ability to define and use the Vocabulary words identified in the selections. The copying masters in this booklet are arranged in the same sequence as the selections in the Student Edition.

These worksheets extend students' study of their Vocabulary words in a variety of ways. In some cases, sentences may describe circumstances or events not found in a selection, in order to provide students with additional practice with context clues. Other acquisition strategies presented in these worksheets are

- creating word maps
- identifying word roots, prefixes, and suffixes
- analyzing root words and word origins
- associating synonyms and antonyms
- examining multiple meanings

Learning how to use a dictionary is a key skill in helping students master new vocabulary. On page viii is a diagram of a simplified dictionary entry with its parts labeled. You may want to point out that syllabication—dividing words into parts to facilitate pronunciation—appears in most dictionary entries. The pronunciation key below the sample dictionary entry lists common words to help students sound out phonetic spellings in dictionary entries. The pronunciation guide on page ix lists words that have common vowel or consonant sounds but have different spellings for those sounds.

Cumulative Vocabulary Reviews

Each end-of-collection Cumulative Vocabulary Review reinforces selected Vocabulary words in that Student Edition collection and preceding collections.

Answer Key

The Answer Key provides answers to all objective questions on the worksheets, as well as models or guidelines for students' responses to open-ended questions and activities.

NAME _____ CLASS _____ DATE _____

How to Use a Dictionary

This is the entry word. It's the word you look up.

These marks indicate the secondary and primary accents.

This is the phonetic spelling of the entry word. It tells you how to pronounce metamorphosis. Use the key below to help you sound out the word.

Here you'll find other forms of the entry word, such as the plural.

met·a·mor·pho·sis [met′ə·môr′fə·sis] *n.*, **metamorphoses 1.** In lower animals, a series of complete changes in body form that take place from birth to the adult stage. **2.** A complete or very obvious change: We watched the *metamorphosis* of the tadpole into a frog. *syns.* change, transformation

This is a sample sentence using the entry word.

This abbreviation tells what part of speech the entry word is.*

Synonyms of the word are listed right after syn.

These are two definitions of the entry word.

This key lists the letters and symbols in phonetic spellings. The words shown have the sounds represented by the letters or symbols.

Pronunciation Key

a	add, map	n	nice, tin	v	vain, eve
ā	ace, rate	ŋ	ring, song	w	win, away
ä	palm, father	ō	open, so	y	yet, yearn
b	bat, rub	ô	order, jaw	yōō	fuse, few
ch	check, catch	oi	oil, boy	z	zest, muse
d	dog, rod	ōō	took, full	zh	vision, pleasure
e	end, pet	ōō	pool, food	ə	the schwa, an unstressed vowel representing the sound spelled a in about e in listen i in pencil o in melon u in circus
ē	equal, tree	ou	pout, now		
f	fit, half	p	pit, stop		
g	go, log	r	run, poor		
h	hope, hate	s	see, pass		
i	it, give	sh	sure, rush		
ī	ice, write	t	talk, sit		
j	joy, ledge	th	thin, both		
k	cool, take	th	this, bathe		
l	look, rule	u	up, done		
m	move, seem	û	burn, term		

*Key to Abbreviations: *n.* noun; *v.* verb; *adj.* adjective; *adv.* adverb; *prep.* preposition; *pron.* pronoun; *interj.* interjection; *conj.* conjunction; *syn.* synonym.

Vocabulary Development

NAME _____ CLASS _____ DATE _____

Pronunciation and Spelling Guide

Use this table to sound out the word parts, or syllables, of unfamiliar Vocabulary words. Notice that the sounds in many words can be formed by a variety of letters or letter combinations.

The sound	in	is spelled as—	The sound	in	is spelled as—
/a/	add	cat, laugh, plaid	/ô/	dog	for, more, roar, ball, walk, dawn, fault, broad, ought
/ā/	age	game, rain, day, gauge	/oi/	oil	noise, toy
/ä/	palm	ah, father, dark, heart, honor, pot	/oo/	took	foot, would, wolf, pull
/b/	bat	big, cabin, rabbit	/o͞o/	pool	cool, lose, soup, through, rude, due, fruit, drew, canoe
/ch/	check	chop, march, catch, nature, mention			
/d/	dog	dig, bad, ladder, called	/ou/	out	ounce, now, bough
/e/	egg	end, met, ready, any, said, says, friend, bury, guess	/p/	put	pin, cap, happy
			/r/	run	red, car, hurry, wrist, rhyme
/ē/	equal	she, eat, see, people, key, field, machine, receive, piano, city	/s/	see	sit, scene, loss, listen, city, psychology
/f/	fit	five, offer, cough, half, photo	/sh/	rush	shoe, sure, ocean, special, machine, mission, lotion, pension, conscience
/g/	go	gate, bigger, vague, ghost			
/h/	hot	hope, who	/t/	top	tan, kept, better, walked, caught
/i/	it	inch, hit, pretty, employ, been, busy, guitar, damage, women, myth, here, dear	/th/	thin	think, cloth
			/th̸/	this	these, clothing
			/u/	up	cut, butter, some, flood, does, young
/ī/	ice	item, fine, pie, high, buy, try, dye, eye, height, island, aisle	/ʉ/	burn	turn, bird, work, early, journey, herd
/j/	joy	jump, gem, magic, cage, edge, soldier, graduate, exaggerate	/v/	very	vote, over, of
			/w/	win	wait
			/y/	yet	year, onion
/k/	keep	king, cat, lock, chorus, account	/yo͞o/	use	cue, few, youth, view, beautiful
/l/	look	let, ball	/z/	zoo	zebra, lazy, buzz, was, scissors
/m/	move	make, hammer, calm, climb, condemn			
			/zh/	vision	pleasure, garage, television
/n/	nice	new, can, funny, know, gnome, pneumonia	/ə/		about, listen, pencil, melon, circus
/ŋ/	ring	thing, tongue			
/ō/	open	oh, over, go, oak, grow, toe, though, soul, sew			

Vocabulary Development **ix**

NAME _____ CLASS _____ DATE _____

VOCABULARY DEVELOPMENT

Contents of the Dead Man's Pocket
Jack Finney

Synonyms and Antonyms

Below are ten word pairs. The first word in each pair is a Vocabulary word. For each numbered pair, write **S** in the blank if the second word in the pair is a synonym of the Vocabulary word or **A** if the word is an antonym. You may want to use a dictionary or a thesaurus for this activity.

_____ 1. projection : recess

_____ 2. discarding : abandoning

_____ 3. confirmation : refutation

_____ 4. exhalation : inhalation

_____ 5. imperceptibly : obviously

_____ 6. rebounded : ricocheted

_____ 7. interminable : incessant

_____ 8. irrelevantly : extraneously

_____ 9. incomprehensible : unfathomable

_____ 10. unimpeded : restricted

Prefixes

All of the Vocabulary words above have prefixes. These word parts have meaning and can change the definition of a root word. Identify the meanings of the prefixes as they are used in the Vocabulary words above. Write the meaning of the prefix in the space provided. The first one has been done for you.

Prefix	Meaning
pro-	before, forward
1. *dis-*	
2. *con-* (*com-*)	
3. *ex-*	
4. *im-* (*in-*, *ir-*)	
5. *re-*	
6. *un-*	

Some of the prefixes above can be added to a root to create the word whose definition is provided below. Write the correct word on the line provided. The prefix is given to help you.

EXAMPLE: *pro-* refuse to permit _____prohibit_____

dis- 7. cease; stop _____

ir- 8. not able to be gotten back _____

ex- 9. go beyond _____

re- 10. bring into existence again _____

NAME _____ CLASS _____ DATE _____

VOCABULARY DEVELOPMENT

Double Daddy • Diary of a Mad Blender • The Child's View of Working Parents
Penny Parker • Sue Shellenbarger • Cora Daniels

Etymologies

Etymology refers to the history of a word, its origins in earlier languages. By becoming familiar with a word's etymology, you can increase your vocabulary power.

Match each Vocabulary word with its correct etymology by writing the Vocabulary word on the line provided. You may want to use a dictionary for help with this exercise. In the dictionary the abbreviation or abbreviations preceding a word's definition reveal the etymology of the word. For example, *OE* means "Old English." If you do not know what a particular abbreviation means, look up the word in the dictionary. (Some dictionaries have abbreviation keys at the beginning or end of the book.)

| phenomenon | chronic | trekked | splicing | integrate |
| colleague | conviction | maximizes | autonomy | poignant |

_____ 1. from the Latin word meaning "one chosen along with another"

_____ 2. from the Afrikaans word meaning "to draw," as when a horse draws, or pulls, a cart

_____ 3. from the Greek word meaning "independence"

_____ 4. from the Latin word meaning "to prick"

_____ 5. from the Greek word meaning "to appear"

_____ 6. from the Latin word meaning "to make whole; renew"

_____ 7. from the Latin word meaning "great"

_____ 8. from the Latin word meaning "proof; demonstration"

_____ 9. from the Greek word meaning "time"

_____ 10. from the Middle Dutch word meaning "to split"

Now, choose four of the Vocabulary words above. On the lines provided, write a brief explanation of how the word's origin and its meaning today are connected.

11. _____

12. _____

13. _____

14. _____

NAME _____ CLASS _____ DATE _____

VOCABULARY DEVELOPMENT

The Leap
Louise Erdrich

Related Meanings

For each group of words below, cross out the word whose meaning or part of speech is different from that of the Vocabulary word (in boldface) and the other two words. Then, on the lines provided, explain your choice. You may want to use a dictionary or a thesaurus for this exercise.

EXAMPLE: a. magazines   b. books   c. tabloids   d. ~~transmit~~

Magazines, books, and tabloids are nouns that name forms of media, whereas transmit is a verb that means "send or cause to go from one place to another."

1. a. **encroaching**   b. barrier   c. advancing   d. progressing

2. a. cemetery   b. **commemorates**   c. remembers   d. memorializes

3. a. **generate**   b. sensitive   c. initiate   d. produce

4. a. luminosity   b. **radiance**   c. elaborate   d. brilliance

5. a. emancipating   b. imprisoning   c. **extricating**   d. unbinding

6. a. educate   b. **illiterate**   c. uneducated   d. unschooled

7. a. **constricting**   b. restraining   c. tightening   d. releasing

8. a. permanent   b. cautious   c. shy   d. **tentative**

Vocabulary Development **3**

NAME _____ CLASS _____ DATE _____

VOCABULARY DEVELOPMENT

The Pedestrian
Ray Bradbury

Question and Answer

Answer the following questions about "The Pedestrian," using context clues to show that you understand the meaning of the italicized Vocabulary words.

1. Does the story *manifest* its eerie subject matter right away? _____

2. Which activity does the police car consider *regressive:* watching television or walking at night? _____

3. Does Mr. Mead *manifest* fear right away when the police car arrives? _____

4. Which could be described as *intermittent* in the story: the sound of people laughing or the silence? _____

5. Which is *ebbing* in the story: television viewing or crime? _____

6. Which would be a *regressive* event in the culture described in the story: repairing the sidewalks or eliminating the last police car? _____

7. What is it about the police car that suggests an *antiseptic*? _____

8. Could the pedestrian traffic at night be described as *intermittent*? _____

4 *Vocabulary Development*

NAME _____ CLASS _____ DATE _____

CUMULATIVE VOCABULARY REVIEW, COLLECTION 1

Sentence Completion

Complete each sentence by using examples, details, or definitions that show you understand the meaning of the italicized Vocabulary word.

EXAMPLE: A *chronic* complainer _has a habit of always finding something wrong._

1. The iron beam formed a *projection* that _____

2. The letter was *confirmation* _____

3. After a great *exhalation* _____

4. Moving almost *imperceptibly,* _____

5. Tom's arm *rebounded* _____

6. To Leonard Mead it was *incomprehensible* _____

7. One *phenomenon* of nature is _____

8. In the editing room, Semantha began *splicing* _____

9. Robert e-mailed his *colleague* _____

10. Someone who has a *conviction* _____

11. Careful preparation *maximizes* _____

12. To be *illiterate* is to _____

Vocabulary Development **5**

NAME _____ CLASS _____ DATE _____

13. In Washington, D.C., a monument *commemorates* _____
_____

14. Dark clouds *generate* _____
_____

15. Despite wearing a blindfold, Harry Avalon might have seen the blue *radiance* because _____
_____

16. A town or city might seem *constricting* because _____
_____

17. To Leonard Mead the dog squads seemed *intermittent* because _____
_____

18. Crime is *ebbing* when _____
_____

19. You would use an *antiseptic* to _____
_____

20. Leonard Mead was assumed to be showing signs of *regressive* behavior because _____
_____

Matching Synonyms

Match each Vocabulary word in column A with its synonym from column B.

A	B
_____ 1. manifest	a. abandoning
_____ 2. tentative	b. endless
_____ 3. extricating	c. touching
_____ 4. autonomy	d. unobstructed
_____ 5. discarding	e. journeyed
_____ 6. interminable	f. unify
_____ 7. unimpeded	g. releasing
_____ 8. trekked	h. reveal
_____ 9. integrate	i. hesitant
_____ 10. poignant	j. independence

6 *Vocabulary Development*

NAME _____ CLASS _____ DATE _____

VOCABULARY DEVELOPMENT

Everyday Use
Alice Walker

Question and Answer

Each of the following questions has an italicized Vocabulary word. Answer the question, and then explain your answer on the lines provided.

EXAMPLE: Asalamalakim is described as stocky. Does that mean he is a good businessman? _No_
Explanation: _It means that he is heavily built, sturdy, and short._

1. Does Dee *sidle* up to people as Maggie does? _____
   Explanation: _____

2. Suppose that Dee behaves in a sneaky manner and that Maggie behaves in an open, honest manner. Which one would be *furtive*? _____
   Explanation: _____

3. Can you picture yourself *cowering* before the narrator? _____
   Explanation: _____

4. If people were to *oppress* you, would they be acting fairly toward you? _____
   Explanation: _____

5. The narrator believes in the practical application of heritage. Would that be considered one of her personal *doctrines*? _____
   Explanation: _____

6. When Dee finished *rifling* through the trunk, would the trunk's contents likely be straightened up or messed up? _____
   Explanation: _____

Now, work with a partner to create three questions that use your Vocabulary words. Write these questions on a separate sheet of paper. On another sheet of paper, answer these three questions in complete sentences. Then, exchange your questions (not your answers) with another pair of students to test their vocabulary strength.

Vocabulary Development **7**

NAME _____ CLASS _____ DATE _____

VOCABULARY DEVELOPMENT

Two Kinds
Amy Tan

Context Clues

Read the sentences below. Using context clues and definitions from the Vocabulary words as a guide, circle the word in parentheses that correctly completes the sentence. Underline any context clues that help you arrive at your answer.

EXAMPLE: My parents entered the concert hall (*listlessly,* (*nonchalantly*)), masking their concern about whether I'd do well.

1. The piano student (*dawdled, lamented*) over her assignment, wasting time by daydreaming.

2. Her performance was a (*betrayal, fiasco*), but she had to admit that her failure resulted from a lack of practice.

3. The string quartet had a (*discordant, mesmerizing*) effect on me, fascinating me with its harmonies and somber mood.

4. She was a noisy child, banging on the keyboard and filling the room with (*stricken, discordant*) sounds.

5. The parents had great hopes that their son would be a concert pianist and felt a certain (*betrayal, prodigy*) when he chose a career as a building inspector.

6. "How disappointing!" (*lamented, dawdled*) the teacher. He regretted spending so much time on such a bored and grumpy student.

7. The guitarist's face took on a (*stricken, mesmerizing*) expression, as if every chord caused him great heartbreak.

8. Because the musicians played (*listlessly, nonchalantly*), the concert lacked energy and the audience went to sleep.

9. After listening to the young violinist, the maestro pronounced her to be a true (*fiasco, prodigy*) with an unusual talent and a rare genius.

10. She was indifferent to praise, for she was quite confident of her talent and accepted it (*nonchalantly, listlessly*).

8 *Vocabulary Development*

NAME _____ CLASS _____ DATE _____

VOCABULARY DEVELOPMENT

By Any Other Name
Santha Rama Rau

Analogies

Love is like a rose—it must be cultivated in order to flourish. In this comparison an analogy is being made. An **analogy** expresses a similarity between two things.

An analogy shows the relationship between two pairs of words. The relationship may be stated in a sentence or expressed using symbols (":" and "::," meaning "is to" and "as"). There are many ways in which the two words in a given pair can be related. Four ways are presented in the following chart.

Relationship	Example	Explanation	Analogy	Translation
synonym	funny : humorous	*Funny* means the same thing as *humorous*.	funny : humorous :: odd : strange	*Funny* is to *humorous* as *odd* is to *strange*.
antonym	joyful : sorrowful	*Joyful* is the opposite of *sorrowful*.	joyful : sorrowful :: happy : sad	*Joyful* is to *sorrowful* as *happy* is to *sad*.
descriptive	creative : artist	An *artist* can be described as *creative*.	creative : artist :: studious : student	*Creative* is to *artist* as *studious* is to *student*.
related action	revise : writer	*Revising* is an action that a *writer* performs.	revise : writer :: build : carpenter	*Revise* is to *writer* as *build* is to *carpenter*.

Complete the analogy, and then identify the relationship between the two words in each pair. The boldface words are the Vocabulary words.

EXAMPLE: unscrupulous : thief :: _____alert_____ : crossing guard (_____descriptive_____)

1. sad : gloomy :: **tepid** : _____ (_____)

2. wholesome : appetite :: **valid** : _____ (_____)

3. **provincial** : _____ :: urban : city (_____)

4. importance : insignificance :: **peevishness** : _____ (_____)

5. worldly : **insular** :: educated : _____ (_____)

6. observed : noticed :: **intimidated** : _____ (_____)

7. fluttering : leaves :: **palpitating** : _____ (_____)

8. juicy : plum :: **wizened** : _____ (_____)

9. intrigued : bored :: _____ : **precarious** (_____)

10. **sedately** : stately :: _____ : cautiously (_____)

Vocabulary Development **9**

NAME _____ CLASS _____ DATE _____

CUMULATIVE VOCABULARY REVIEW, COLLECTIONS 1–2

Sentence Completion

Complete each sentence by using examples, details, or definitions that show you understand the meaning of the italicized Vocabulary word.

EXAMPLE: For some people a quilt *commemorates* _the life of the person or persons who made it._

1. Mama in "Everyday Use" might be called *illiterate* because _____

2. Compared with her bold sister, Maggie was afflicted by *chronic* _____

3. If a cat was to *sidle* up to you, _____

4. Maggie's glances at her sister were *furtive* because _____

5. Maggie was *cowering* when _____

6. To Wangero the name Dee was *irrelevantly* hers because _____

7. Letting Dee (Wangero) have the quilts would have been a *betrayal* because _____

8. You would be *rifling* through a cabinet if _____

9. A piece of music might be *mesmerizing* because _____

10. Stevie Wonder was called a *prodigy* because _____

11. Jing-mei's mother seemed to *oppress* her by _____

12. Auntie Lindo *lamented* Waverly's talent, but she was really _____

10 *Vocabulary Development*

NAME _____ CLASS _____ DATE _____

13. Someone might appear *stricken* if _____

14. The performance turned into a *fiasco* when _____

15. A new student might be *intimidated* by _____

16. Directions for walking *sedately* would say _____

17. A face that is *wizened* is _____

18. A *valid* identification card is _____

19. Someone might be called *insular* who _____

20. Premila's *peevishness* was evident when _____

Matching Synonyms

Match each Vocabulary word in column A with its synonym from column B.

A	B
_____ 1. tepid	a. casually
_____ 2. provincial	b. lingered
_____ 3. precarious	c. throbbing
_____ 4. dawdled	d. principles
_____ 5. discordant	e. clashing
_____ 6. doctrines	f. unsophisticated
_____ 7. encroaching	g. unstable
_____ 8. palpitating	h. lukewarm
_____ 9. nonchalantly	i. unenergetically
_____ 10. listlessly	j. approaching

Vocabulary Development **11**

NAME _____ CLASS _____ DATE _____

VOCABULARY DEVELOPMENT

The Storyteller
Saki

Related Meanings

For each group of words below, cross out the word whose meaning is different from that of the Vocabulary word (in boldface) and the other two words. You may want to use a dictionary or a thesaurus for this exercise.

EXAMPLE: **a. devious**   b. indirect   c. ~~straightforward~~   d. deceitful

Devious, indirect, and *deceitful* all mean "roundabout." *Straightforward* has an opposite meaning.

1. a. humid   b. muggy   c. **sultry**   d. arid
2. a. endless   b. discontinuous   c. relentless   d. **persistent**
3. a. **diversion** b. focus   c. distraction   d. amusement
4. a. vague   b. determined   c. **resolute**   d. steadfast
5. a. peevish   b. **petulant**   c. docile   d. impatient
6. a. **deplorably**b. purposely   c. horribly   d. terribly
7. a. doubt   b. **conviction** c. certainty   d. creed
8. a. gibe   b. question   c. **retort**   d. quip
9. a. besiege   b. **assail**   c. attack   d. desist

Sentence Writing

Now, on the lines provided, write six original sentences relating to "The Storyteller." In each sentence, use at least one Vocabulary word from the activity above.

1. _____
   _____
2. _____
   _____
3. _____
   _____
4. _____
   _____
5. _____
   _____
6. _____
   _____

12 *Vocabulary Development*

NAME _____ CLASS _____ DATE _____

VOCABULARY DEVELOPMENT

The Cold Equations
Tom Godwin

Word Maps

Fill in the ovals below with a synonym, an antonym, and the connotation of each of the Vocabulary words, as well as with the dictionary definition and a sentence using the word correctly. For the word's connotation, write whether you think it is *positive*, *negative*, or *neutral*, and be sure that the sentence you write reflects this connotation. The first word map has been partially completed for you.

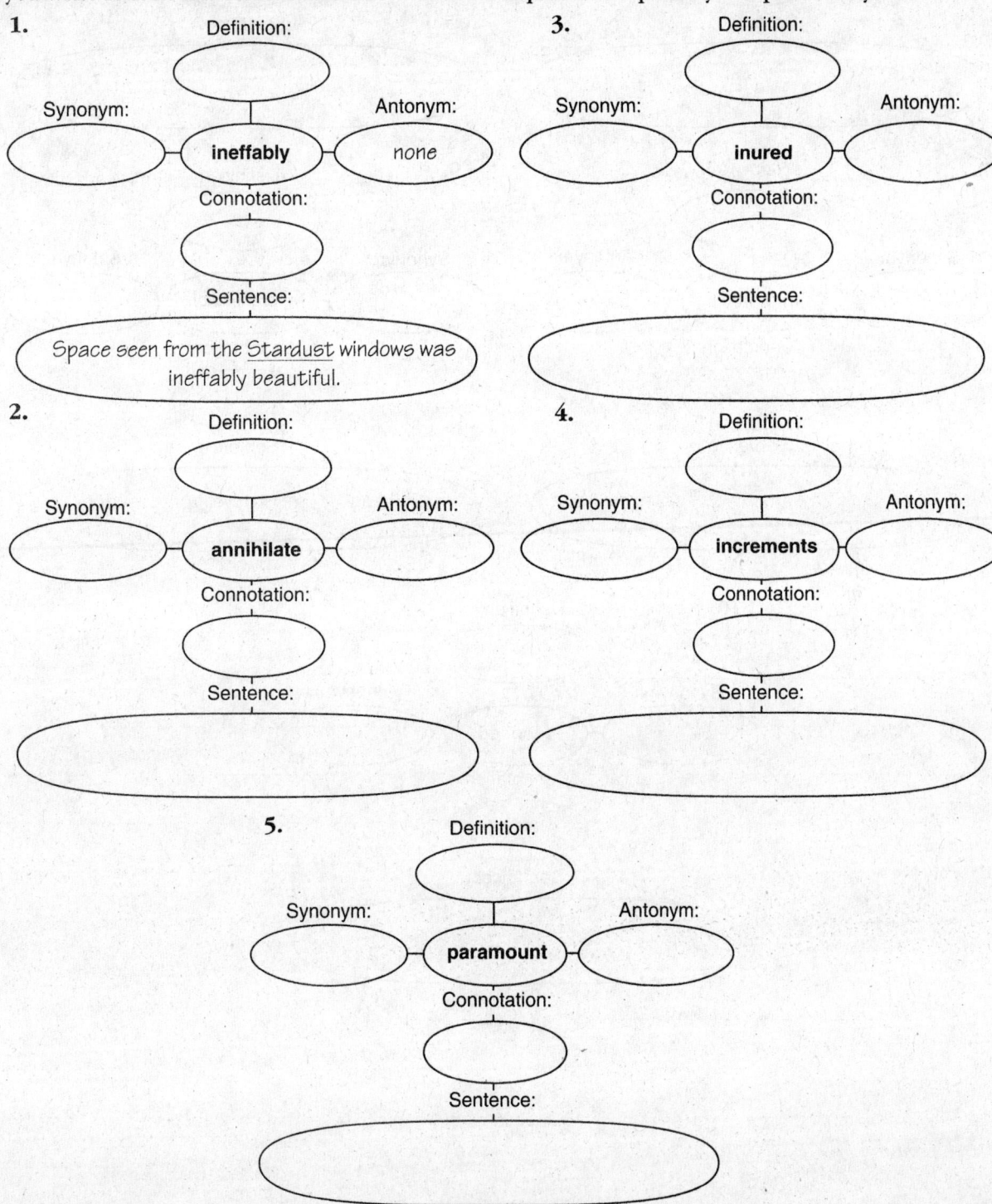

1. **ineffably**
   - Definition:
   - Synonym:
   - Antonym: none
   - Connotation:
   - Sentence: Space seen from the Stardust windows was ineffably beautiful.

2. **annihilate**
   - Definition:
   - Synonym:
   - Antonym:
   - Connotation:
   - Sentence:

3. **inured**
   - Definition:
   - Synonym:
   - Antonym:
   - Connotation:
   - Sentence:

4. **increments**
   - Definition:
   - Synonym:
   - Antonym:
   - Connotation:
   - Sentence:

5. **paramount**
   - Definition:
   - Synonym:
   - Antonym:
   - Connotation:
   - Sentence:

Vocabulary Development **13**

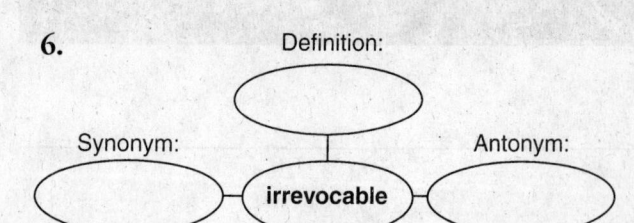

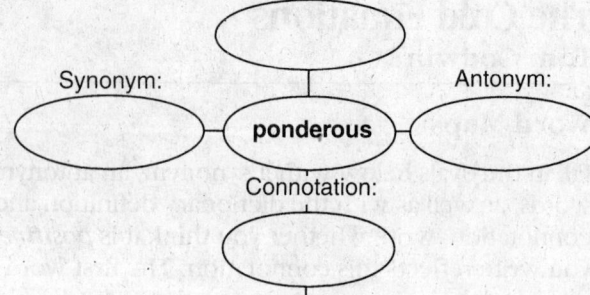

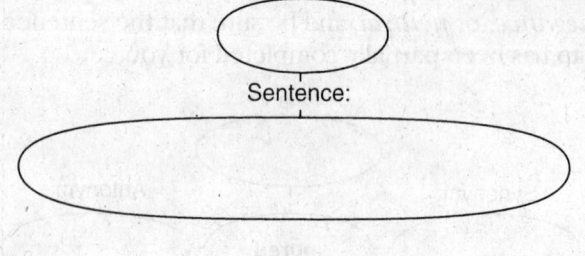

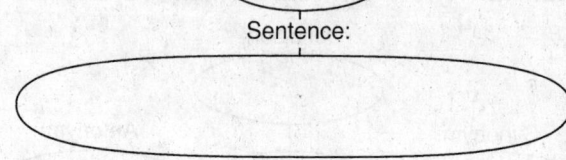

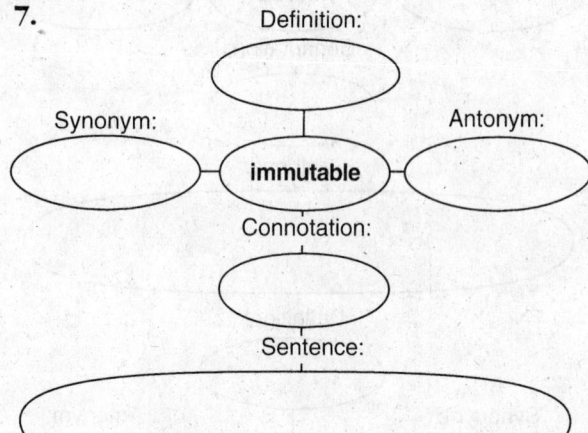

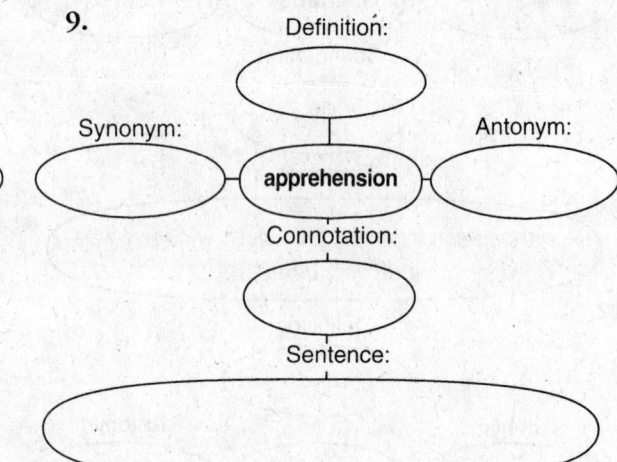

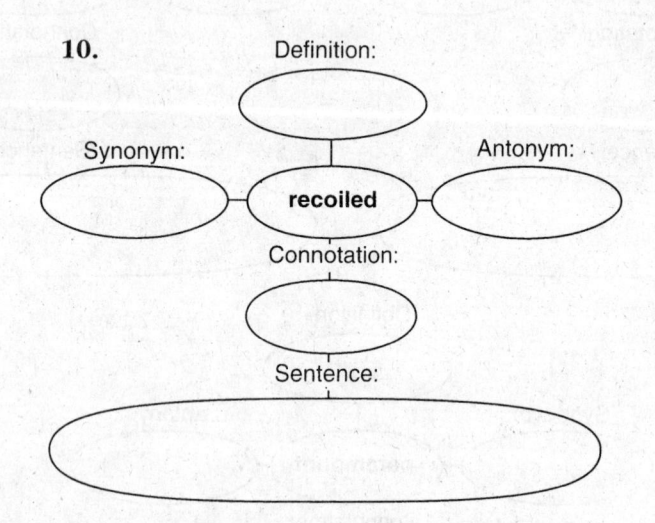

NAME _____ CLASS _____ DATE _____

6. irrevocable — Definition, Synonym, Antonym, Connotation, Sentence

7. immutable — Definition, Synonym, Antonym, Connotation, Sentence

8. ponderous — Definition, Synonym, Antonym, Connotation, Sentence

9. apprehension — Definition, Synonym, Antonym, Connotation, Sentence

10. recoiled — Definition, Synonym, Antonym, Connotation, Sentence

14 *Vocabulary Development*

NAME _____ CLASS _____ DATE _____

VOCABULARY DEVELOPMENT

Taste—The Final Frontier
Esther Addley

Question and Answer

Answer the following questions about "Taste—The Final Frontier," using context clues to show that you understand the meaning of the italicized Vocabulary words.

1. What is the final frontier that has been *breached*? _____
   _____

2. How might food be made *palatable* for astronauts flying their missions? _____
   _____

3. What might cause food to become *rancid*? _____
   _____

4. Why were the Russian astronauts close to *mutiny*? _____
   _____

5. What effect did an *impoverished* space agency have on the food for Russian astronauts? ____
   _____

6. What is an astronaut's *habitat*? _____
   _____

7. What might a *judicious* cook do with raw ingredients? _____
   _____

8. According to the selection, what substance affects astronauts' *metabolism* in space? ____
   _____

9. What might be an *arresting* idea regarding life on Mars? _____
   _____

Vocabulary Development **15**

NAME _____ CLASS _____ DATE _____

VOCABULARY DEVELOPMENT

Typhoid Fever *from* Angela's Ashes
Frank McCourt

Related Meanings

In each of the following word groups, the Vocabulary word is in boldface type. Cross out the word whose meaning or part of speech is different from the meanings or parts of speech of the other words in the group. Then, write a sentence or two explaining your choice.

EXAMPLE: a. persuasive **b. potent** c. ~~feeble~~ d. effective

Although all the words are adjectives, feeble means "weak," and the other words mean "strong; powerful; compelling."

1. a. influenced   b. discouraged   c. convinced   d. **induced**

_____

_____

2. a. hostility   b. **torrent**   c. stream   d. flood

_____

_____

3. a. **clamoring**   b. juggling   c. circling   d. crash

_____

_____

Using Words Correctly

Each sentence below uses a Vocabulary word (in boldface). If the Vocabulary word has been used correctly, write **C** on the line before each sentence. If it has been used incorrectly, write **I**, and on the lines that follow, explain the error.

EXAMPLE: ___I___ After the nurse left, Frank **induced** his appetite for literature.
Induced means "persuaded; led someone on." Indulged means "gave in to; satisfied a wish."

_____ 1. As the sun set, the highwayman was **clamoring** up the wall of the inn.

_____

_____

_____ 2. Perhaps a magic **potent** could have healed Patricia.

_____

_____

_____ 3. The landlord's daughter must have felt a **torrent** of passion for the highwayman.

_____

_____

16 *Vocabulary Development*

NAME _____ CLASS _____ DATE _____

CUMULATIVE VOCABULARY REVIEW, COLLECTIONS 1–3

Sentence Completion

Complete each sentence by using examples, details, or definitions that show you understand the meaning of the italicized Vocabulary word.

EXAMPLE: A ballet dancer or athlete might become *inured* ___to tired and aching muscles.___

1. A *torrent* of rain _____

2. A *persistent* noise _____

3. The bachelor's story was a *diversion* because _____

4. Someone who behaves *deplorably* _____

5. To make a *retort*, you _____

6. The children found the bachelor's story *mesmerizing* because _____

7. The bachelor thought the children would *assail* the aunt because _____

8. Because Marilyn had *breached* the limits of EDS regulations, _____

9. The command center's orders were *irrevocable*, meaning that _____

10. The recipe said to add the flour to the batter in *increments*, so Thomas _____

11. The stowaway *recoiled* when _____

12. Marilyn's situation was *poignant* because _____

Vocabulary Development **17**

NAME _____ CLASS _____ DATE _____

13. An elephant's footsteps are *ponderous* compared with _____

14. Gerry's voice was filled with *apprehension* when _____

15. Food that is *palatable* is _____

16. Something *rancid* would taste _____

17. Astronauts who began a *mutiny* would _____

18. A *habitat* designed for a teenager today _____

19. The use of flavorings is *judicious* when _____

20. If your *metabolism* is working, then _____

Matching Synonyms

Match each Vocabulary word in column A with its synonym from column B.

A	B
____ 1. potent	a. determined
____ 2. sultry	b. indescribably
____ 3. resolute	c. unchangeable
____ 4. paramount	d. strong
____ 5. annihilate	e. poor
____ 6. conviction	f. sweltering
____ 7. arresting	g. certainty
____ 8. impoverished	h. interesting
____ 9. ineffably	i. destroy
____ 10. immutable	j. dominant

18 *Vocabulary Development*

NAME _____ CLASS _____ DATE _____

VOCABULARY DEVELOPMENT

Catch the Moon
Judith Ortiz Cofer

Context Clues

Using context clues and definitions of the Vocabulary words as a guide, circle the word in parentheses that correctly completes each sentence. Underline any context clues that help you determine the answer.

EXAMPLE: The judge had released Luis into the (*barrio*, (*custody*)) of his father, who would be legally responsible for his son's behavior.

1. One of the cars Mr. Cintrón worked on was a (*vintage, sarcastic*) Mustang, one of the first ever made by Ford.

2. Looking at the Mustang, Luis taunted his father with a (*vintage, sarcastic*) comment, saying that the car looked like a reject from a rodeo.

3. Although some people preferred a car with a white finish, Luis preferred (*ebony, vintage*) because the dark finish did not show dirt as easily.

4. Most of the junkyard was filled with old (*relics, ebony*) that had meaning for Mr. Cintrón but for no one else.

Matching Antonyms

Match each Vocabulary word in column A with its antonym from column B. You may want to use a dictionary or a thesaurus for this exercise.

A	B
_____ 1. relics	a. pleasing
_____ 2. harassing	b. sincere
_____ 3. ebony	c. novelties
_____ 4. sarcastic	d. recent
_____ 5. vintage	e. assembled
_____ 6. dismantled	f. white

Vocabulary Development **19**

Vocabulary Development

The Bass, the River, and Sheila Mant
W. D. Wetherell

Etymologies

Etymology refers to the history of a word, its origins in earlier languages. By becoming familiar with a word's etymology, you can increase your vocabulary power.

Match each Vocabulary word below with its correct etymology by writing the Vocabulary word on the line provided. You may want to use a dictionary to help you with this exercise. In the dictionary the abbreviation or abbreviations preceding a word's definition reveal its etymology. For example, *OE* means "Old English." If you do not understand a particular abbreviation, look it up in the dictionary. (Some dictionaries have abbreviation keys at the beginning or end of the book.)

| denizens | antipathy | conspicuous | quizzical | surreptitiously |
| pensive | filial | concussion | luminous | dubious |

_____ 1. from the Latin word meaning "to weigh or consider"

_____ 2. from the Latin word meaning "to take away secretly"

_____ 3. from the Latin word meaning "light" (the noun)

_____ 4. from the Latin word meaning "to look at"

_____ 5. from the Greek word meaning "opposition in feeling"

_____ 6. probably from the Latin word meaning "what sort of person or thing?"

_____ 7. from the Latin word meaning "to shake violently"

_____ 8. from the Latin word meaning "uncertain"

_____ 9. from the Latin word meaning "son" or "daughter"

_____ 10. from the Latin word meaning "within"

Now, choose five of the Vocabulary words above. On the lines provided, write a brief explanation of how the word's origin and its contemporary meaning are connected.

11. _____

12. _____

13. _____

14. _____

15. _____

NAME _____ CLASS _____ DATE _____

VOCABULARY DEVELOPMENT

And of Clay Are We Created
Isabel Allende

Synonyms and Antonyms

Below are ten word pairs. The first word in each pair is a Vocabulary word. Write **S** if the second word in the pair is a synonym of the Vocabulary word or **A** if the word is an antonym. You may want to use a dictionary for this exercise.

_____ 1. ingenuity : stupidity

_____ 2. resignation : resistance

_____ 3. commiserate : sympathize

_____ 4. pandemonium : chaos

_____ 5. subterranean : underground

_____ 6. presentiments : forebodings

_____ 7. tenacity : fickleness

_____ 8. magnitude : immensity

_____ 9. equanimity : agitation

_____ 10. fortitude : faintheartedness

Prefixes

A **prefix** is a word part added to the beginning of a root word. A prefix changes a word's meaning and may change its part of speech. Use a dictionary to complete the chart below. Find the root of each Vocabulary word, the definition and part of speech of the root, and the definition of each prefix. Finally, tell what the definition of the Vocabulary word is, and give its part of speech. Some of the chart has been filled in for you.

Vocabulary Word	Root Word and Definition	Part of Speech of Root Word	Prefix and Definition	Definition and Part of Speech of Vocabulary Word
1. subterranean	terra, "earth"			
2. presentiments				
3. pandemonium				

NAME _____ CLASS _____ DATE _____

VOCABULARY DEVELOPMENT

The Man in the Water
Roger Rosenblatt

Making Word Connections

1. Look up the noun *flail* in a dictionary. Describe a flail.
   _____

   Now, explain how the verb *flail* is related to the noun.
   _____

2. Use a dictionary to look up the two word parts that make up *extravagant,* and write the meanings of each part below.

   extra- _____ *vagari* _____

3. *Abiding* comes from a Middle English word meaning "remain." Look up the noun *abode,* which is related to the same Middle English word. Explain how the noun *abode* and the adjective *abiding* are related.
   _____

4. One meaning of the noun *pit* is "place where animals are put to fight." (You might think of a lion pit or a snake pit.) How are the noun *pit* and the past tense verb *pitted* related?
   _____

5. Use an unabridged dictionary to find the meanings of the three word parts that make up *implacable,* and write the meaning of each part below.

   im- _____ *placare* _____ *-able* _____

Using Words Correctly

Each sentence below uses a Vocabulary word (in boldface). If the Vocabulary word has been used correctly, write **C** on the line before each sentence. If it has been used incorrectly, write **I,** and on the lines that follow, explain the error.

EXAMPLE: ___I___ The reporters **anonymously** decided that the man was the greatest modern hero.

Anonymous means that a person's identity is not known. Unanimous means that all agree.

_____ 1. The passenger was **flailing** his arms as the helicopter moved in to throw him a line.
   _____

_____ 2. An **abiding** lesson learned from the disaster is that humans can rise above their own need to survive. _____

_____ 3. Americans are **implacable** because they are always changing their opinions.
   _____

22 *Vocabulary Development*

NAME _____ CLASS _____ DATE _____

VOCABULARY DEVELOPMENT

If Decency Doesn't, Law Should Make Us Samaritans • Good Samaritans U.S.A. Are Afraid to Act
Gloria Allred *and* Lisa Bloom • Ann Sjoerdsma

Connotations

A word's **denotation** is its objective dictionary definition, or literal meaning. **Connotations** are meanings suggested by the word. They can have strong positive or negative effects on people's emotions. Some words, such as *table*, do not evoke any emotion and are considered neutral in connotation.

Decide which of the Vocabulary words below have positive connotations, which have negative connotations, and which are neutral. In the space before the number for each word, write **P** for positive, **N** for negative, or **O** for neutral. Then, on the lines that follow, explain your answer by using examples or personal experiences.

EXAMPLE: __P__ civilized I think of a civilized person as one who is educated and law-abiding.

_____ 1. allegations _____

_____ 2. depraved _____

_____ 3. liability _____

_____ 4. rationalizations _____

_____ 5. solidarity _____

_____ 6. callous _____

_____ 7. feigning _____

_____ 8. immunity _____

_____ 9. construed _____

_____ 10. indemnifies _____

Vocabulary Development **23**

NAME _____ CLASS _____ DATE _____

CUMULATIVE VOCABULARY REVIEW, COLLECTIONS 1–4

Sentence Completion

Complete each sentence by using examples, details, or definitions that show you understand the meaning of the italicized Vocabulary word.

EXAMPLE: If a law *indemnifies* a person, _____it protects the person._____

1. Luis was *resolute* _____

2. The *denizens* of juvenile hall _____

3. Someone who *dismantled* a computer printer would have _____

4. Sheila Mant had a *pensive* look when _____

5. Dating Sheila Mant filled the narrator with *apprehension* because _____

6. Because of the size of the *concussion,* the fisher knew _____

7. The narrator of "The Bass, the River, and Sheila Mant" expressed *resignation* when _____

8. To express *filial* devotion, _____

9. The mudslide in Colombia was of such *magnitude* that _____

10. Rolf Carlé showed *tenacity* in _____

11. *Extricating* Azucena from the mud _____

12. Viewers looked *stricken* when _____

24 *Vocabulary Development*

NAME _____ CLASS _____ DATE _____

13. *Pandemonium* might occur if _____

14. *Presentiments* might cause a person to _____

15. It would be appropriate to *commiserate* with someone when _____

16. You might be *pitted* against nature if _____

17. A person who is *flailing* _____

18. *Rationalizations* for not helping someone in trouble might include ___

19. If you heard *allegations* of cheating, you would _____

20. To show social *solidarity*, _____

Matching Synonyms

Match each Vocabulary word in column A with its synonym from column B.

A	B
_____ 1. construed	a. troubling
_____ 2. extravagant	b. mocking
_____ 3. callous	c. black
_____ 4. harassing	d. doubtful
_____ 5. dubious	e. obvious
_____ 6. conspicuous	f. showy
_____ 7. sarcastic	g. immoral
_____ 8. ebony	h. unfeeling
_____ 9. depraved	i. pretending
_____ 10. feigning	j. interpreted

Vocabulary Development **25**

NAME _____ CLASS _____ DATE _____

VOCABULARY DEVELOPMENT

Lamb to the Slaughter
Roald Dahl

Using Words Correctly

Each sentence below uses a Vocabulary word (in boldface). If the Vocabulary word has been used correctly, write **C** on the line before each sentence. If it has been used incorrectly, write **I**, and on the lines that follow, explain the error.

EXAMPLE: __I__ It was **depraved** of you to bring such a lovely gift to the party.
Depraved means "immoral; corrupt"; you wouldn't show appreciation for a gift by calling someone depraved.

_____ 1. The upcoming final examination had filled the student body with **anxiety.**

_____ 2. The barking of the dogs, the shouting of the children, the constant arrival of guests — all added up to a **placid** day.

_____ 3. I **luxuriated** in the terrible loss my team suffered on Saturday afternoon.

_____ 4. The nurse spoke calmly and reassuringly as she **administered** the flu shot.

_____ 5. The visitor had soon gained a reputation for not following through on his **premises.**

_____ 6. After she won the race, we all ran up to offer **consoling** words in celebration of her victory.

_____ 7. We appreciated your **hospitality,** especially since we arrived on such short notice.

26 *Vocabulary Development*

NAME _____ CLASS _____ DATE _____

VOCABULARY DEVELOPMENT

R.M.S. Titanic
Hanson W. Baldwin

Analogies

An **analogy** shows the relationship between two pairs of words. The relationship may be stated in a sentence or expressed by using symbols (":" and "::," meaning "is to" and "as"). There are many ways in which two words in a given pair can be related. Five ways are presented in the following chart.

Relationship	Example	Explanation	Analogy	Translation
similarity	potato : yam	A *potato* is similar to a *yam*.	potato : yam :: glove : mitten	*Potato* is to *yam* as *glove* is to *mitten*.
antonym	cold : hot	*Cold* is the opposite of *hot*.	cold : hot :: liquid : solid	*Cold* is to *hot* as *liquid* is to *solid*.
synonym	gentle : calm	*Gentle* is a synonym of calm.	gentle : calm :: smooth : even	*Gentle* is to *calm* as *smooth* is to *even*.
related action	write : author	An *author* writes.	write : author :: swim : fish	*Write* is to *author* as *swim* is to *fish*.
cause	gift : joy	A *gift* causes *joy*.	gift : joy :: joke : laughter	*Gift* is to *joy* as *joke* is to *laughter*.

On the line after each colon, write a word that correctly completes the analogy. On the line between the parentheses, write the relationship between the word pairs. You may use a dictionary or a thesaurus. The boldface words are the Vocabulary words.

EXAMPLE: musician : perform :: athlete : _____run_____ ___(related action)___

1. agile : nimble :: **perfunctory** : _____ (_____)
2. **superlative** : best :: joyous : _____ (_____)
3. **pertinent** : applicable :: irrelevant : _____ (_____)
4. aimed : hunter :: **poised** : _____ (_____)
5. effectively : successfully :: **vainly** : _____ (_____)
6. raised : lowered :: **corroborated** : _____ (_____)
7. **garbled** : clear :: hurried : _____ (_____)
8. **recriminations** : countercharges :: labor : _____ (_____)
9. **quelled** : dictator :: baked : _____ (_____)
10. disruption : interference :: **ascertain** : _____ (_____)

Vocabulary Development **27**

NAME _____ CLASS _____ DATE _____

VOCABULARY DEVELOPMENT

from Into Thin Air
Jon Krakauer

Analogies

"The writing process is like building a house," says your teacher. With this statement your teacher is making an **analogy**, a way of expressing a relationship between two things. The relationship in this case is one of similarity—between building a house and writing a paper. The pairs of words in the following chart show some of the other ways in which words can be related.

Word Pairs	Relationship
catastrophe : disaster	synonym
innocent : guilty	antonym
eloquent : speaker	description

For the pairs of words below, identify the relationship of the words in the first pair by writing *synonym, antonym,* or *description* on the first line. On the second line, write a word that correctly completes the analogy. Be sure the relationship between the words in the second word pair is the same as that between the words in the first pair. You may want to use a dictionary and a thesaurus. The words in boldface type are the Vocabulary words.

EXAMPLE: ___antonym___ arduous : easy :: ethereal : ___earthly___

1. _____ **deteriorate** : improve :: subtract : _____

2. _____ brilliant : light :: **innocuous** : _____

3. _____ **notorious** : unknown :: truthful : _____

4. _____ theorize : **speculate** :: speak : _____

5. _____ summit : **apex** :: diligent : _____

6. _____ fierce : attack :: **crucial** : _____

7. _____ destructive : creative :: **benign** : _____

8. _____ develop : mature :: **traverse** : _____

9. _____ **jeopardize** : secure :: whisper : _____

10. _____ clever : suggestion :: **tenuous** : _____

28 *Vocabulary Development*

NAME _____ CLASS _____ DATE _____

VOCABULARY DEVELOPMENT

Explorers Say There's Still Lots to Look For
Helen O'Neill

Related Meanings

For each group of words below, cross out the word whose meaning is different from that of the Vocabulary word (in boldface). You may want to use a dictionary or thesaurus for this exercise.

EXAMPLE: a. **pertinent**   b. important   c. relevant   d. ~~deceitful~~

1. a. dream   b. reality   c. **illusion**   d. vision
2. a. stranded   b. isolated   c. relentless   d. **marooned**
3. a. **nudged**   b. bumped   c. pushed   d. amused
4. a. humor   b. oddity   c. **whimsy**   d. worry
5. a. steerer   b. **navigator** c. plotter   d. spoiler

Sentence Writing

Now, on the lines provided, write five original sentences relating to "Explorers Say There's Still Lots to Look For." In each sentence, use at least one Vocabulary word from the activity above.

1. _____

2. _____

3. _____

4. _____

5. _____

Vocabulary Development **29**

NAME _____ CLASS _____ DATE _____

VOCABULARY DEVELOPMENT

Notes from a Bottle
James Stevenson

Word Maps

Fill in the ovals below with a synonym, an antonym, and the connotation of each of the Vocabulary words, as well as with the dictionary definition and a sentence using the word correctly. For the word's connotation, write whether you think it is *positive*, *negative*, or *neutral*, and be sure that the sentence you write reflects this connotation. The first word map has been partially completed for you.

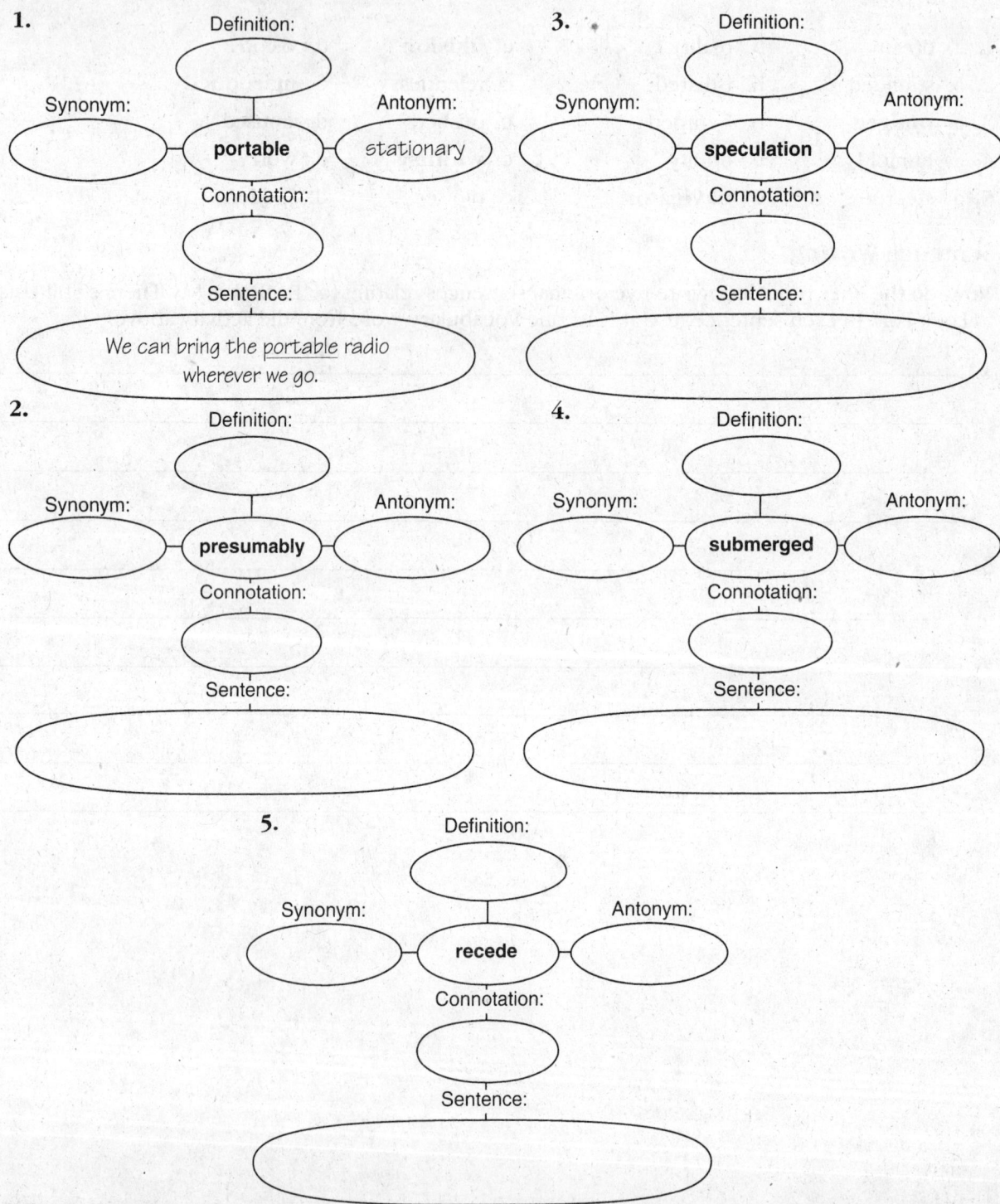

1. **portable**
   - Definition:
   - Synonym:
   - Antonym: stationary
   - Connotation:
   - Sentence: We can bring the portable radio wherever we go.

2. **presumably**
   - Definition:
   - Synonym:
   - Antonym:
   - Connotation:
   - Sentence:

3. **speculation**
   - Definition:
   - Synonym:
   - Antonym:
   - Connotation:
   - Sentence:

4. **submerged**
   - Definition:
   - Synonym:
   - Antonym:
   - Connotation:
   - Sentence:

5. **recede**
   - Definition:
   - Synonym:
   - Antonym:
   - Connotation:
   - Sentence:

NAME _____ CLASS _____ DATE _____

CUMULATIVE VOCABULARY REVIEW, COLLECTIONS 1–5

Sentence Completion

Complete each sentence by using examples, details, or definitions that show you understand the meaning of the italicized Vocabulary word.

EXAMPLE: The *portable* radio _allows us to listen to music wherever we go._

1. On the *placid* lake _____

2. Mary Maloney loved to *luxuriate* _____

3. The blow to Patrick Maloney was *administered* _____

4. The *superlative* qualities of the *Titanic* _____

5. *Titanic* crew members went below to *ascertain* _____

6. To arrive at the *apex* means _____

7. Sometimes rescuing injured climbers may *jeopardize* _____

8. *Marooned* for months, _____

9. The *navigator* is depended upon for _____

10. The *clamoring* crowd _____

11. If the weather begins to *deteriorate*, climbers on Mount Everest _____

12. Their *hospitality* was demonstrated by _____

Vocabulary Development **31**

NAME _____ CLASS _____ DATE _____

13. They *corroborated* the story by _____

14. A *pertinent* fact is _____

15. The *recriminations* began _____

16. The *vintage* automobile _____

17. Around the *premises* could be found _____

18. The *garbled* message _____

19. With a *quizzical* look _____

20. In my *anxiety* I _____

Matching Synonyms

Match each Vocabulary word in column A with its synonym from column B.

A	B
____ 1. consoling	a. cross
____ 2. induced	b. fruitlessly
____ 3. vainly	c. impatient
____ 4. fortitude	d. comforting
____ 5. quelled	e. courage
____ 6. petulant	f. harmless
____ 7. traverse	g. subdued
____ 8. subterranean	h. underground
____ 9. benign	i. bumped
____ 10. nudged	j. persuaded

32 *Vocabulary Development*

NAME _____ CLASS _____ DATE _____

VOCABULARY DEVELOPMENT

Through the Tunnel
Doris Lessing

Using Word Parts to Build Meaning

For each Vocabulary word, create your own definition by combining the meanings given in the boxes below for each word's root, prefix, and suffix. If there is more than one meaning given for any word part, underline the meaning that best suits the word you are defining. Finally, write a sentence using the word in the proper context. The first item has been partially completed for you as an example.

Vocabulary Word	Root	Prefix	Suffix
1. contrition	*tritus*, past participle of *terere*, "to rub"	*con-*, "with, together"	*-ion*, "result, act, or condition of"

Meaning: con– (together) + tritus (to rub) + –ion (act of): act of rubbing together.
Sentence:

| 2. supplication | *plicare*, "to fold" | *sup- (sub-)*, "under" | *-ion*, "result, act, or condition of" |

Meaning:
Sentence:

| 3. defiant | *defier*, "to defy" | | *-ant*, "has; shows; does" |

Meaning:
Sentence:

| 4. inquisitive | *quaerere*, "to seek" | *in-*, "into; toward; on" | *-ive*, "belonging to; quality of" |

Meaning:
Sentence:

| 5. minute | *minuere*, "to lessen" | | *-tus*, "degree of; characteristic of" |

Meaning:
Sentence:

| 6. incredulous | *credere*, "to believe" | *in-*, "no; not; without" | *-ous*, "having; full of; characterized by" |

Meaning:
Sentence:

Vocabulary Development **33**

NAME _____ CLASS _____ DATE _____

VOCABULARY DEVELOPMENT

Coming of Age, Latino Style •
Vision Quest • Crossing a Threshold to Adulthood
Cindy Rodriguez • from *Encyclopaedia Britannica*
• Jessica Barnes

Related Meanings

In each of the following word groups, the Vocabulary word is in boldface type. Cross out the word whose meaning or part of speech is different from the meanings or parts of speech of the other words in the group.

1. a. **indigenous**   b. native   c. original   d. foreigner
2. a. lonely   b. **solitary**   c. isolated   d. unique
3. a. **vigil**   b. watch   c. guard   d. evening
4. a. frequent   b. noticeable   c. obscure   d. **predominant**
5. a. remarkable   b. impressive   c. humble   d. **formidable**
6. a. **inevitable**   b. unlikely   c. unavoidable   d. certain

Suffixes

A suffix is a word part added to the end of a root word. A suffix changes a word's meaning and can change its part of speech. Use a dictionary for help completing the chart below. Find the root of each Vocabulary word, the definition and part of speech of the root, and the definition of each suffix. Finally, tell what the definition of each Vocabulary word is, and give its part of speech. Some parts of the chart have been filled out for you.

Vocabulary Word	Root Word and Definition	Part of Speech of Root Word	Suffix and Definition	Definition and Part of Speech of Vocabulary Word
1. indigenous			–ous, "having; full of"	
2. solitary	*solus,* "alone"	adjective		
3. predominant			–ant, "has; shows; does"	

34 *Vocabulary Development*

NAME _____ CLASS _____ DATE _____

VOCABULARY DEVELOPMENT

The Masque of the Red Death
Edgar Allan Poe

Making Meanings with Synonyms

Use a dictionary or a thesaurus to find a synonym for each Vocabulary word below. Then, write a sentence or two using context clues that make the meaning of the synonym clear.

EXAMPLE: formidable _____impressive_____

Sentence: His explanation was so clear that his command of the subject could be called impressive.

1. profuse _____ Sentence: _____

2. sagacious _____ Sentence: _____

3. contagion _____ Sentence: _____

4. imperial _____ Sentence: _____

5. emanating _____ Sentence: _____

6. sedate _____ Sentence: _____

7. pervaded _____ Sentence: _____

8. cessation _____ Sentence: _____

9. propriety _____ Sentence: _____

10. tangible _____ Sentence: _____

Vocabulary Development **35**

NAME _____ CLASS _____ DATE _____

CUMULATIVE VOCABULARY REVIEW, COLLECTIONS 1–6

Sentence Completion

Complete each sentence by using examples, details, or definitions that show you understand the meaning of the italicized Vocabulary word.

EXAMPLE: The *imperial* palace _was a majestic sight._

1. I felt *contrition* after _____

2. A look of *supplication* means _____

3. An *indigenous* coming-of-age tradition _____

4. A *solitary* journey involves _____

5. A *vigil* is _____

6. With an *inquisitive* look _____

7. Such a *formidable* presence _____

8. In a display of *ingenuity*, _____

9. With an *implacable* stare _____

10. The young man *surreptitiously* _____

11. The *luminous* glow _____

12. The *predominant* emotion at a wedding _____

36 *Vocabulary Development*

NAME _____ CLASS _____ DATE _____

13. The Red Death caused *profuse* bleeding that _____
_____

14. The Prince thought to defy the *contagion* by _____
_____

15. The *cessation* of hostilities _____
_____

16. Laughter *pervaded* _____
_____

17. A *sagacious* person _____
_____

18. The *notorious* criminal _____
_____

19. I *nudged* the person next to me by _____
_____

20. The *crucial* decision _____
_____

Matching Synonyms

Match each Vocabulary word in column A with its synonym from column B.

A	B
_____ 1. antipathy	a. calm
_____ 2. speculate	b. guess
_____ 3. sedate	c. composure
_____ 4. incredulous	d. responsibility
_____ 5. defiant	e. harmless
_____ 6. emanating	f. emerging
_____ 7. equanimity	g. disbelieving
_____ 8. minute	h. challenging
_____ 9. innocuous	i. dislike
_____ 10. liability	j. tiny

Vocabulary Development **37**

NAME _____ CLASS _____ DATE _____

VOCABULARY DEVELOPMENT

Night Calls
Lisa Fugard

Connotations

A word's **denotation** is its objective dictionary definition, or literal meaning. Many words also have connotations. **Connotations** are meanings suggested by the word. They can have strong positive or negative effects on people's emotions. For example, *thin* and *scrawny* both denote "light weight." However, many people would consider it a compliment to be called thin but would be offended if referred to as scrawny. Some words, such as *table*, do not evoke any emotion and are considered neutral in connotation.

Decide which of the Vocabulary words below have positive connotations, which have negative connotations, and which are neutral. In the space before the number for each word, write **P** for positive, **N** for negative, or **O** for neutral. Then, on the lines that follow, explain your answer by using examples or personal experiences.

EXAMPLE: __P__ formidable __Something that is formidable is strong and impressive, which signal positive traits.__

_____ 1. inevitably

_____ 2. avid

_____ 3. indigenous

_____ 4. opulent

_____ 5. adamant

_____ 6. abutting

_____ 7. lauding

_____ 8. tremulous

_____ 9. patina

NAME _____ CLASS _____ DATE _____

VOCABULARY DEVELOPMENT

Call of the Wild—Save Us!
Norman Myers

Related Meanings

For each group of words below, cross out the word whose meaning or part of speech is different from that of the Vocabulary word (in boldface) and the other two words.

EXAMPLE: a. cheering   b. praising   **c. lauding**   d. ~~declining~~

1. a. eclipses   b. **habitats**   c. surroundings   d. environments
2. a. exterminated   b. extinguished   c. patina   d. **extinct**
3. a. **impoverishment** b. need   c. bruise   d. poverty
4. a. decline   b. **degradation**   c. destruction   d. blossoming
5. a. moral   b. excitable   c. **ethical**   d. just
6. a. elimination   b. preservation   c. protection   d. **conservation**
7. a. **bereft**   b. needy   c. lacking   d. satisfied
8. a. consumption   b. buying   c. **consumerism** d. contagion
9. a. beginning   b. **terminal**   c. final   d. concluding
10. a. actual   b. tentative   c. true   d. **veritable**

Sentence Writing

Now, on the lines provided, write five original sentences relating to "Call of the Wild—Save Us!" In each sentence, use at least one Vocabulary word from the activity above.

1. _____
   _____

2. _____
   _____

3. _____
   _____

4. _____
   _____

5. _____
   _____

NAME _____ CLASS _____ DATE _____

VOCABULARY DEVELOPMENT

A Very Old Man with Enormous Wings
Gabriel García Márquez

Antonyms

For each item below, choose the word whose meaning is opposite that of the italicized Vocabulary word. Write the letter of the antonym in the blank provided. You may need a dictionary or a thesaurus to find the correct antonym.

_____ 1. The *stench* from the dead crabs was overpowering.
   a. stink   b. odor   c. perfume

_____ 2. *Impeded* by the fence, the angel had to stay in the chicken coop.
   a. restrained   b. freed   c. bothered

_____ 3. Even though they felt *magnanimous*, they still did not clean out the chicken coop.
   a. selfish   b. generous   c. noble

_____ 4. The angel did not seem to be deserving of *reverence*.
   a. respect   b. dishonor   c. awe

_____ 5. Elisenda spent her money on a pair of *frivolous* satin shoes.
   a. useful   b. trivial   c. ridiculous

_____ 6. The angel suffered many *impertinences* committed by the child.
   a. indignities   b. tributes   c. reprimands

_____ 7. Despite Father Gonzaga's cautions, the *ingenuous* people continued to listen to all opinions.
   a. wise   b. innocent   c. naive

_____ 8. The angel showed *prudence* and did not eat the mothballs.
   a. caution   b. ingenuity   c. carelessness

_____ 9. The people thought that the angel would cause a great *cataclysm*.
   a. calm   b. upheaval   c. disaster

_____ 10. The angel's arrival was *providential* for Pelayo and Elisenda.
   a. divine   b. unfortunate   c. lucky

_____ 11. The woman who had been changed into a spider told her story with sincere *affliction*.
   a. distress   b. suffering   c. joy

_____ 12. The owners of the house did not *lament* when the woman who had changed into a spider crushed the angel.
   a. rejoice   b. mourn   c. grieve

40 Vocabulary Development

NAME _____ CLASS _____ DATE _____

CUMULATIVE VOCABULARY REVIEW, COLLECTIONS 1–8

Sentence Completion

Complete each sentence by using examples, details, or definitions that show you understand the meaning of the italicized Vocabulary word.

EXAMPLE: A *terminal* threat to wildlife _is one that could bring about the widespread loss of many species._

1. In "Night Calls" the *conservation* effort requires _____

2. *Adamant,* the girl's aunt _____

3. The *tremulous* wail _____

4. *Abutting* our yard _____

5. An *avid* reader _____

6. If you are *lauding* a movie you saw, you _____

7. Norman Myers argues that we destroy wildlife *habitats* _____

8. A species becomes *extinct* when _____

9. An *impoverishment* of our ecosystem occurs _____

10. A world *bereft* of wildlife is _____

11. *Prudence* would dictate that _____

12. It was *providential* that _____

Vocabulary Development **41**

NAME _____ CLASS _____ DATE _____

13. The *affliction* caused _____

14. I *lament* that _____

15. The young man's *impertinences* caused _____

16. It was quite *ingenuous* of you to _____

17. Our progress was *impeded* by _____

18. It was easy to be *magnanimous* because _____

19. The *opulent* costume _____

20. A society obsessed by *consumerism* _____

Matching Synonyms

Match each Vocabulary word in column A with its synonym from column B.

A	B
_____ 1. ethical	a. true
_____ 2. presumably	b. suitability
_____ 3. cataclysm	c. unavoidably
_____ 4. tangible	d. stink
_____ 5. degradation	e. moral
_____ 6. inevitably	f. disbelieving
_____ 7. stench	g. decline
_____ 8. veritable	h. disaster
_____ 9. propriety	i. touchable
_____ 10. incredulous	j. probably

42 *Vocabulary Development*

NAME _____ CLASS _____ DATE _____

VOCABULARY DEVELOPMENT

Where Have You Gone, Charming Billy?
Tim O'Brien

Synonyms and Antonyms

Below are four word pairs. The first word in each pair is a Vocabulary word. For each numbered pair, write **S** in the blank if the second word in the pair is a synonym of the Vocabulary word or **A** if the word is an antonym. You may need a dictionary or a thesaurus for this activity.

_____ 1. stealth : secretiveness

_____ 2. diffuse : focused

_____ 3. agile : awkward

_____ 4. valiantly : bravely

Writing Sentences

Now, on the lines provided, write seven original sentences relating to "Where Have You Gone, Charming Billy?" In each sentence, use a Vocabulary word from the list below.

| stealth | diffuse | skirted | agile |
| inertia | valiantly | consolation | |

1. _____

2. _____

3. _____

4. _____

5. _____

6. _____

7. _____

Vocabulary Development **43**

NAME _____ CLASS _____ DATE _____

VOCABULARY DEVELOPMENT

The War Escalates • Dear Folks •
from Declaration of Independence from the War in Vietnam
Paul Boyer • Kenneth W. Bagby • Martin Luther King, Jr.

Making Word Connections

1. You've learned that the Vocabulary word *facile* is an adjective meaning "easy." Using a dictionary if necessary, find a noun that is related to *facile*. Write the noun on the lines below, and explain how the two words are related.

   _____
   _____

2. Look up the etymology of the Vocabulary word *aghast*. Write the origin of this word below.

   _____
   _____

   Now, using a dictionary if necessary, think of another word with the same origin, and use it in a sentence on the lines below.

   _____
   _____

Using Words Correctly
Each sentence below uses a Vocabulary word (in boldface). If the Vocabulary word has been used correctly, write **C** on the line before each sentence. If it has been used incorrectly, write **I,** and on the lines that follow, explain the error.

_____ 1. I found it impossible to take *initiative* in such a restrictive, uncreative atmosphere.

   _____

_____ 2. The **rehabilitation** of the neighborhood can be achieved with the proper planning and a high level of cooperation.

   _____

_____ 3. I felt a great deal of **compassion** at the news that your team took first place in the debate competition.

   _____

_____ 4. She was so good at **manipulation** that the audience refused to follow her directives.

   _____

44 *Vocabulary Development*

NAME _____ CLASS _____ DATE _____

VOCABULARY DEVELOPMENT

The Sword in the Stone *from* Le Morte d'Arthur
Sir Thomas Malory, *retold by* Keith Baines

Related Meanings

In each of the following word groups, the Vocabulary word is in boldface type. Cross out the word whose meaning or part of speech is different from the meanings or parts of speech of the other words in the group. Then, write a sentence or two explaining your choice.

EXAMPLE: **a. aghast**   **b. horrified**   **c. stricken**   **d. torment**
Aghast, horrified, and stricken are all adjectives that describe a state of shock at something terrible that has happened. Torment has a similar negative connotation, but it is not an adjective; it is either a noun or a verb.

1. a. **confronted**   b. challenged   c. faced   d. avoided

2. a. engraving   b. **inscription**   c. etching   d. painting

3. a. promise   b. reward   c. declaration   d. **oath**

4. a. common   b. resolute   c. **ignoble**   d. lowborn

5. a. **tumultuous**   b. spirited   c. compassionate   d. wild

6. a. kingdom   b. **realm**   c. throne   d. domain

7. a. crowning   b. enthronement   c. initiative   d. **coronation**

Vocabulary Development **45**

NAME _____ CLASS _____ DATE _____

VOCABULARY DEVELOPMENT

The Tale of Sir Launcelot du Lake *from* Le Morte d'Arthur
Sir Thomas Malory, *retold by* Keith Baines

Etymologies

Etymology refers to the history of a word, its origins in earlier languages. By becoming familiar with a word's etymology, you can increase your vocabulary power.

Match each Vocabulary word below with its correct etymology by writing the Vocabulary word on the line provided. You may want to use a dictionary for help with this exercise. In the dictionary the abbreviation or abbreviations preceding a word's definition reveal its etymology. For example, *OE* means "Old English." If you do not understand a particular abbreviation, look it up in the dictionary. (Some dictionaries have abbreviation keys at the beginning or end of the book.)

diverted	fidelity	oblige	champion
adversary	sovereign	wrath	

_____ 1. from the Latin word meaning "above; over"

_____ 2. from the Latin word meaning "to turn aside"

_____ 3. from the Old English word meaning "wroth; angry"

_____ 4. from the Latin word meaning "to bind"

_____ 5. from the Latin word meaning "field; place for games"

_____ 6. from the Latin word meaning "faith"

_____ 7. from the Latin word meaning "turned opposite"

Now, on the lines provided, write a brief explanation of how each word's origin and its contemporary meaning are connected.

1. _____
2. _____
3. _____
4. _____
5. _____
6. _____
7. _____

NAME _____ CLASS _____ DATE _____

CUMULATIVE VOCABULARY REVIEW, COLLECTIONS 1–9

Sentence Completion

Complete each sentence by using examples, details, or definitions that show you understand the meaning of the italicized Vocabulary word.

EXAMPLE: The *stealth* of warfare involves _sly behavior and secret tactics._

1. Paul Berlin's *diffuse* fears _____

2. The soldiers showed *consolation* _____

3. *Valiantly* the defenders of the fort _____

4. By definition a *frivolous* request is _____

5. A *patina* of green _____

6. With great *reverence* _____

7. The animal's *terminal* illness _____

8. King argued for the *rehabilitation* _____

9. King claimed that the world was *aghast* _____

10. King argued that the United States must take the *initiative* _____

11. The *predominant* mood of the crowd _____

12. With a bit of *whimsy,* _____

Vocabulary Development **47**

NAME _____ CLASS _____ DATE _____

13. Was it an *illusion*, or _____
_____

14. The congregation at St. Paul's, on leaving the church, was *confronted* _____
_____

15. Under an *oath*, Sir Kay _____
_____

16. It was unheard of for someone of *ignoble* blood _____
_____

17. At a *coronation* _____
_____

18. The knights of the Round Table *diverted* _____
_____

19. With *wrath* Sir Launcelot _____
_____

20. When the waters began to *recede*, _____
_____

Matching Synonyms

Match each Vocabulary word in column A with its synonym from column B.

	A		B
_____	1. skirted	**a.**	lively
_____	2. agile	**b.**	sympathy
_____	3. facile	**c.**	engraving
_____	4. manipulation	**d.**	wild
_____	5. compassion	**e.**	kingdom
_____	6. inscription	**f.**	avoided
_____	7. tumultuous	**g.**	devotion
_____	8. realm	**h.**	compel
_____	9. fidelity	**i.**	control
_____	10. oblige	**j.**	easy

48 *Vocabulary Development*

NAME _____ CLASS _____ DATE _____

VOCABULARY DEVELOPMENT

The Brute
Anton Chekhov

Synonyms and Antonyms

Below are seven word pairs. The first word in each pair is a Vocabulary word. Write **S** if the second word in the pair is a synonym of the Vocabulary word or **A** if the word is an antonym. You may want to use a dictionary for this exercise.

_____ 1. indisposed : healthy

_____ 2. emancipation : liberation

_____ 3. malicious : kindly

_____ 4. insinuate : suggest

_____ 5. incoherent : clear

_____ 6. impudence : disrespect

_____ 7. impunity : liability

Using Words Correctly

Each sentence below contains a boldface Vocabulary word. On the line before each sentence, write **C** if the word has been used correctly or **I** if the word has been used incorrectly.

EXAMPLE: ___C___ We **diverted** the twins' attention by telling them that the new toys were in the basement.

_____ 1. I'm feeling **indisposed,** so I would be happy to participate in the track-and-field competition.

_____ 2. It was an act of **emancipation** to force the animals into the pen.

_____ 3. The plot the evil schemer hatched was clearly **malicious** in its intent.

_____ 4. We're going to be forced to hire an exterminator to **insinuate** the house against pests.

_____ 5. The **incoherent** lecture made the lesson crystal clear to the class.

_____ 6. I was shocked that a young person would show such **impudence** before an adult.

_____ 7. My **impunity** to the disease will allow me to continue the exploration.

Vocabulary Development **49**

NAME _____ CLASS _____ DATE _____

VOCABULARY DEVELOPMENT

Julius Caesar in an Absorbing Production
John Mason Brown

Making Meaning with Antonyms

Use a dictionary or a thesaurus to find an antonym for each Vocabulary word below. Then, write a sentence in which you use both the Vocabulary word and the antonym. Your sentences should use context clues that make the meaning of the antonyms clear.

EXAMPLE: malicious ____kindly____ Sentence: We thought the stranger might be malicious, but she was actually *kindly* and helpful.

1. gaunt _____ Sentence: _____

2. vitality _____ Sentence: _____

3. surly _____ Sentence: _____

4. unorthodox _____ Sentence: _____

5. sinister _____ Sentence: _____

6. reticent _____ Sentence: _____

7. perplexed _____ Sentence: _____

8. idealist _____ Sentence: _____

NAME _____ CLASS _____ DATE _____

CUMULATIVE VOCABULARY REVIEW, COLLECTIONS 1–10

Sentence Completion

Complete each sentence by using examples, details, or definitions that show you understand the meaning of the italicized Vocabulary word.

    EXAMPLE: The proceedings grew so *tumultuous* that the presiding officer was not able to restore order.

1. Mrs. Popov pretended to be *indisposed* _____

2. Smirnov, claiming women to be *malicious*, _____

3. Mrs. Popov felt Smirnov had dared to *insinuate* _____

4. When Mrs. Popov is *incoherent*, _____

5. Smirnov's *impudence* _____

6. The *adamant* instructor _____

7. An act of *emancipation* _____

8. To act with *impunity* _____

9. The *gaunt* stage on which Welles's production was mounted _____

10. The *unorthodox* production _____

11. Brutus can be seen as *perplexed*, _____

12. The *vitality* of the performance _____

Vocabulary Development **51**

NAME _____ CLASS _____ DATE _____

13. The *surly* waiter _____

14. A feeling of *inertia* _____

15. An *idealist* _____

16. The details of the *sinister* plan _____

17. The *reticent* student _____

18. The *sovereign* _____

19. The *relics* that were discovered _____

20. The grant of *immunity* _____

Matching Synonyms

Match each Vocabulary word in column A with its synonym from column B.

A	B
_____ 1. adversary	a. secrecy
_____ 2. champion	b. calm
_____ 3. adamant	c. opponent
_____ 4. stealth	d. guesswork
_____ 5. cataclysm	e. comforting
_____ 6. inevitable	f. support
_____ 7. sedate	g. insistent
_____ 8. speculation	h. disaster
_____ 9. presumably	i. probably
_____ 10. consoling	j. unavoidable

52 *Vocabulary Development*

Answer Key

Collection 1   Plot and Setting • Synthesizing Sources

Contents of the Dead Man's Pocket, page 1

Synonyms and Antonyms
1. A
2. S
3. A
4. A
5. A
6. S
7. S
8. S
9. S
10. A

Prefixes
1. away; apart; the opposite of
2. with; together
3. out
4. not. Use *im-* before *b*, *m*, or *p*; use *in-* before all letters except *b*, *l*, *m*, *p*, or *r*.
5. again
6. not
7. discontinue
8. irretrievable
9. exceed
10. reproduce

Double Daddy • *Diary of a Mad Blender* • *The Child's View of Working Parents*, page 2

Etymologies
1. colleague
2. trekked
3. autonomy
4. poignant
5. phenomenon
6. integrate
7. maximizes
8. conviction
9. chronic
10. splicing

(Explanations will vary. Sample responses follow.)

11. *phenomenon:* The word comes from the Greek word for "appear." Today a *phenomenon* is an event, fact, or circumstance that can be seen.
12. *trekked:* The word comes from the Afrikaans word meaning "to draw," as when a horse pulls a cart. Today *trekked* means "have gone on a journey."
13. *integrate:* The word comes from the Latin word meaning "to make whole; renew." Today the word means "combine" or "unify."
14. *poignant:* The word comes from the Latin word meaning "to prick." Today *poignant* means "emotionally moving; touching."

The Leap, page 3

Related Meanings
1. b. barrier. *Encroaching, advancing,* and *progressing* are verbs that mean "moving forward"; *barrier* is a noun that means "obstacle."
2. a. cemetery. *Commemorates, remembers,* and *memorializes* are verbs that refer to the memory of someone or something, but *cemetery* is a noun meaning "place where bodies are buried."
3. b. sensitive. *Generate, initiate,* and *produce* are verbs that mean "bring into being; make happen." *Sensitive* is an adjective meaning "of the senses."
4. c. elaborate. *Luminosity, radiance,* and *brilliance* have to do with light or brightness, but *elaborate* means "complicated."
5. b. imprisoning. *Emancipating, extricating,* and *unbinding* mean "letting go; releasing"; *imprisoning* means "restricting."
6. a. educate. *Illiterate, uneducated,* and *unschooled* are adjectives meaning "unable to read and write." *Educate* is a verb meaning "train; teach."
7. d. releasing. *Constricting, restraining,* and *tightening* all have to do with the idea of limiting or confining, whereas *releasing* has to do with letting go or freeing.
8. a. permanent. *Cautious, shy,* and *tentative* are adjectives meaning "timid; hesitant," but *permanent* is an adjective meaning "fixed."

The Pedestrian, page 4

Question and Answer
(Responses will vary. Sample responses follow.)

1. No. At first it seems that Mr. Mead is out for a walk in a quiet place, but it becomes clear in a few paragraphs that there is more to it than that.
2. Walking at night is considered regressive because everyone is expected to be indoors watching television.
3. No. Mr. Mead calmly answers the questions. He is a trusting person who doesn't believe that he is doing anything wrong.
4. The sound of people laughing is intermittent, and the silence seems to be all-pervasive.
5. Crime is ebbing because everyone is too busy watching television to be committing crimes.
6. Repairing the sidewalks would be regressive because it suggests that people were intending to use them. In this culture no one is supposed to be walking.
7. The smell of the police car suggests an antiseptic.
8. No. The pedestrian traffic at night could not be described as intermittent because there are no pedestrians other than Mr. Mead.

Vocabulary Development **53**

Cumulative Vocabulary Review, Collection 1, page 5

Sentence Completion
(Answers will vary. Sample answers follow.)
1. The iron beam formed a *projection* that stuck out three feet from the building.
2. The letter was *confirmation* that Yassir had been accepted by the college.
3. After a great *exhalation*, Tom realized he'd been holding his breath.
4. Moving almost *imperceptibly*, the lion crept toward the feeding gazelles.
5. Tom's arm *rebounded* after striking the window without breaking it.
6. To Leonard Mead it was *incomprehensible* that the police would arrest him for walking.
7. One *phenomenon* of nature is the rising and setting of the sun.
8. In the editing room, Semantha began *splicing* tape of the old home movies.
9. Robert e-mailed his *colleague* about the new office procedure.
10. Someone who has a *conviction* has a strong belief in something.
11. Careful preparation *maximizes* your chances of doing well on a test.
12. To be *illiterate* is to be unable to read or write.
13. In Washington, D.C., a monument *commemorates* the life of Abraham Lincoln.
14. Dark clouds *generate* a feeling of gloom at the beginning of a storm.
15. Despite wearing a blindfold, Harry Avalon might have seen the blue *radiance* because the light was very bright.
16. A town or city might seem *constricting* because it has limited opportunities for work and pleasure.
17. To Leonard Mead the dog squads seemed *intermittent* because he saw them only from time to time.
18. Crime is *ebbing* when there are fewer robberies and murders.
19. You would use an *antiseptic* to clean a wound in order to prevent infection.
20. Leonard Mead was assumed to be showing signs of *regressive* behavior because he went for a walk when people no longer did such things.

Matching Synonyms
1. h
2. i
3. g
4. j
5. a
6. b
7. d
8. e
9. f
10. c

Collection 2 Character • Using Primary and Secondary Sources

Everyday Use, page 7

Question and Answer
(Responses will vary. Sample responses follow.)
1. No. Dee does not react in a shy or sneaky manner, but in an outgoing and direct one.
2. Dee. Dee would be furtive because *furtive* means "sneaky."
3. Yes or no. Some students may find her overbearing, and some may not.
4. No. When people oppress someone, they persecute the person, acting in an unfair and unjust way.
5. Yes. She believes in the practical application of heritage, and a doctrine is a belief or principle.
6. Messed up. *Rifling* means "looking through in a rough manner," so the contents of the trunk would be roughly treated and therefore messed up.

(Questions and answers will vary. Students should write three questions using Vocabulary words. They should answer their questions in complete sentences on a separate sheet of paper.)

Two Kinds, page 8

Context Clues
(In the following answers, words that correctly complete the sentences are italicized. Context clues are underlined.)
1. *dawdled* wasting time; daydreaming
2. *fiasco* failure; lack of practice
3. *mesmerizing* fascinating
4. *discordant* noisy; banging
5. *betrayal* hopes; concert pianist; building inspector
6. *lamented* disappointing; regretted
7. *stricken* heartbreak
8. *listlessly* lacked energy; sleep
9. *prodigy* unusual talent; rare genius
10. *nonchalantly* indifferent; accepted

By Any Other Name, page 9

Analogies

(Responses will vary. Sample responses follow. Analogy relationships are in parentheses.)
1. lukewarm (synonym)
2. excuse (descriptive)
3. country (descriptive)
4. patience (antonym)
5. illiterate (antonym)
6. bullied (synonym)
7. heart (descriptive)
8. prune (descriptive)
9. sturdy (antonym)
10. carefully (synonym)

Cumulative Vocabulary Review, Collections 1–2, page 10

Sentence Completion

(Answers will vary. Sample answers follow.)
1. Mama in "Everyday Use" might be called *illiterate* because she did not receive an education and can't read or write.
2. Compared with her bold sister, Maggie was afflicted by *chronic* shyness.
3. If a cat was to *sidle* up to you, it would move toward you in a shy or sneaky way.
4. Maggie's glances at her sister were *furtive* because she was self-conscious and afraid of her sister.
5. Maggie was *cowering* when she drew fearfully behind her mother as Dee arrived.
6. To Wangero the name Dee was *irrelevantly* hers because it was no longer the name she called herself.
7. Letting Dee (Wangero) have the quilts would have been a *betrayal* because Mama had promised them to Maggie for her wedding.
8. You would be *rifling* through a cabinet if you were searching through it in a rough manner.
9. A piece of music might be *mesmerizing* because it has a beautiful melody and fascinating rhythms.
10. Stevie Wonder was called a *prodigy* because he was extremely talented as a child.
11. Jing-mei's mother seemed to *oppress* her by trying to make her into a genius.
12. Auntie Lindo *lamented* Waverly's talent, but she was really bragging.
13. Someone might appear *stricken* if he or she has seen something shocking or very sad.
14. The performance turned into a *fiasco* when the child began playing so many wrong notes.
15. A new student might be *intimidated* by a mean or insensitive teacher.
16. Directions for walking *sedately* would say to walk in a calm and dignified manner.
17. A face that is *wizened* is wrinkled and dried up.
18. A *valid* identification card is accepted or recognized by authorities.
19. Someone might be called *insular* who is narrow-minded or isolated from his or her surroundings.
20. Premila's *peevishness* was evident when she came into class and told Santha they were going home.

Matching Synonyms

1. h
2. f
3. g
4. b
5. e
6. d
7. j
8. c
9. a
10. i

Collection 3   Narrator and Voice • Generating Research Questions

The Storyteller, page 12

Related Meanings
1. d
2. b
3. b
4. a
5. c
6. b
7. a
8. b
9. d

Sentence Writing

(Sentences will vary. Each original sentence should contain a Vocabulary word used correctly. Sample sentences follow.)
1. The *sultry* air in the cabin caused the passengers to sweat and yawn.
2. The aunt grew tired of the children's *persistent* questions.
3. The aunt's story was not a very successful *diversion* for the children.
4. One child's voice was *resolute* as she sang a silly song.
5. Because of the aunt's *petulant* reply, the bachelor began to tell a story.
6. The aunt had told her story so *deplorably* that the children were bored.

The Cold Equations, page 13

Word Maps

(Responses will vary. Sample responses follow.)

1. *Definition:* indescribably; inexpressibly
   Synonym: indefinably
   Antonym: none
   Connotation: neutral
   Sentence: Space seen from the *Stardust* windows was ineffably beautiful.
2. *Definition:* destroy; demolish
   Synonym: kill
   Antonym: create
   Connotation: negative
   Sentence: The pilot prepared to annihilate the uninhabited planet blocking the flight path of his rescue mission.
3. *Definition:* accustomed to something difficult or painful
   Synonym: hardened
   Antonym: unaccustomed
   Connotation: neutral
   Sentence: The pilot became inured to his difficult duties.
4. *Definition:* small increases in amount
   Synonym: gains
   Antonym: decreases
   Connotation: neutral
   Sentence: His raises came in annual increments of fifty dollars.
5. *Definition:* supreme; dominant
   Synonym: chief
   Antonym: unimportant
   Connotation: positive
   Sentence: Helping the girl was his paramount interest.
6. *Definition:* irreversible; unable to be canceled or undone
   Synonym: unalterable
   Antonym: alterable
   Connotation: negative
   Sentence: The interstellar law is irrevocable.
7. *Definition:* unchangeable; never changing or varying
   Synonym: constant
   Antonym: changeable
   Connotation: neutral
   Sentence: The pilot disliked his immutable routine.
8. *Definition:* heavy, slow-moving, or dull; showing or requiring great effort
   Synonym: labored
   Antonym: fast-moving
   Connotation: negative
   Sentence: Janice thought the science fiction story was boring and ponderous.
9. *Definition:* anxious feeling of foreboding
   Synonym: dread
   Antonym: eagerness
   Connotation: negative
   Sentence: The pilot approached the task with apprehension.
10. *Definition:* retreated or drew back in fear, surprise, or disgust
    Synonym: cringed
    Antonym: confronted
    Connotation: negative
    Sentence: When asked the disturbing question, she recoiled and kept quiet.

Taste—The Final Frontier, page 15

Question and Answer

(Responses will vary. Sample responses follow.)

1. Four decades ago astronauts broke through the final barrier of outer space.
2. The flavor of the food might be improved by using spices.
3. Food that is not eaten but is left to rot would become rancid.
4. The Russian astronauts were ready to rebel because their food was so terrible.
5. The agency couldn't afford good food, and the astronauts were apparently angry.
6. An astronaut's environment is often a space vehicle orbiting the earth.
7. A wise and experienced cook would prepare a delicious meal.
8. Salt has an important effect on how the human body turns food into energy.
9. Some people like the idea of growing food on Mars, but that is not likely to happen soon.

Typhoid Fever from *Angela's Ashes,* page 16

Related Meanings

(Explanations will vary somewhat. Sample explanations follow the correct answer.)

1. b. discouraged; Although all of the words are verbs, *discouraged* means "disheartened; dispirited," but the other words mean "persuaded; prompted."
2. a. hostility; Although all of the words are nouns, *hostility* means "ill will," but the other words mean "outburst; gush."
3. d. crash; *Clamoring, juggling,* and *circling* are all participles, but *crash* is a verb (or a noun).

Using Words Correctly

(Explanations will vary somewhat. Sample explanations follow the correct answer.)

1. I; *Clamor* means "ask; cry out." It is unrelated to the word *climb.*
2. I; *Potent* means "convincing; powerful." It is unrelated to the word *potion.*
3. C

Cumulative Vocabulary Review, Collections 1–3, page 17

Sentence Completion
(Answers will vary. Sample answers follow.)
1. A *torrent* of rain poured from the sky.
2. A *persistent* noise is a noise that continues without stopping.
3. The bachelor's story was a *diversion* because it distracted the children.
4. Someone who behaves *deplorably* behaves very badly.
5. To make a *retort*, you make a quick, sharp reply to someone's comments.
6. The children found the bachelor's story *mesmerizing* because it was the opposite of a "nice," or proper, story.
7. The bachelor thought the children would *assail* the aunt because they had so loved the improper story that they wanted her to tell one like it.
8. Because Marilyn had *breached* the limits of EDS regulations, she had to be ejected from the ship.
9. The command center's orders were *irrevocable*, meaning that they could not be canceled or undone.
10. The recipe said to add the flour to the batter in *increments*, so Thomas added a small amount, then a larger amount, then a still larger amount.
11. The stowaway *recoiled* when she heard the orders to jettison her.
12. Marilyn's situation was *poignant* because she was young, she just wanted to see her brother, she was innocent, and yet she had to die.
13. An elephant's footsteps are *ponderous* compared with those of a cat.
14. Gerry's voice was filled with *apprehension* when he heard Marilyn's voice from the EDS and knew his sister was in danger.
15. Food that is *palatable* is fit to eat.
16. Something *rancid* would taste stale or spoiled.
17. Astronauts who began a *mutiny* would rebel or revolt against authority.
18. A *habitat* designed for a teenager today might include a computer, a bed, and a refrigerator filled with snack food.
19. The use of flavorings is *judicious* when the taste of the flavorings does not overwhelm.
20. If your *metabolism* is working, then your body is converting food into energy and living tissue.

Matching Synonyms
1. d
2. f
3. a
4. j
5. i
6. g
7. h
8. e
9. b
10. c

Collection 4 Comparing Themes • Evaluating Arguments: Pro and Con

Catch the Moon, page 19

Context Clues
1. *vintage* one of the first ever made
2. *sarcastic* taunted
3. *ebony* the dark finish
4. *relics* old; that had meaning

Matching Antonyms
1. c
2. a
3. f
4. b
5. d
6. e

The Bass, the River, and Sheila Mant, page 20

Etymologies
1. pensive
2. surreptitiously
3. luminous
4. conspicious
5. antipathy
6. quizzical
7. concussion
8. dubious
9. filial
10. denizens

(Explanations will vary. Sample responses follow.)
11. *luminous*: The word comes from the Latin word meaning "light," and something that is *luminous* is full of light.
12. *conspicuous*: The word comes from the Latin word meaning "to look at," and something that is *conspicuous* is obvious because it can be observed in some way.
13. *concussion*: The word comes from the Latin word meaning "to shake violently," and a *concussion* is an injury resulting from a violent blow or impact to an organ, especially the brain.
14. *dubious*: The word comes from the Latin word meaning "uncertain," and *dubious* means "have doubts; be doubtful or uncertain."
15. *filial*: The word comes from the Latin word meaning "son" or "daughter," and *filial* today means "of, suitable to, or due from a son or daughter."

And of Clay Are We Created, page 21

Synonyms and Antonyms
1. A
2. A
3. S
4. S
5. S
6. S
7. A
8. S
9. A
10. A

Prefixes
1. Root Word and Definition: *terra*, "earth"; Part of Speech of Root Word: noun; Prefix and Definition: *sub-*, "under"; Definition and Part of Speech of Vocabulary Word: "underground"; adjective
2. Root Word and Definition: *sentiment*, "combination of feelings and opinions"; Part of Speech of Root Word: noun; Prefix and Definition: *pre-*, "before"; Definition and Part of Speech of Vocabulary Word: "forebodings"; noun
3. Root Word and Definition: *daimon*, "demon"; Part of Speech of Root Word: noun; Prefix and Definition: *pan-*, "all"; Definition and Part of Speech of Vocabulary Word: "wildly noisy, chaotic scene"; noun

The Man in the Water, page 22

Making Word Connections
(Sentences will vary. Sample responses follow.)
1. A *flail* is a wooden threshing tool that has a long handle and a thick stick hanging loosely from one end.
   The stout stick swings about freely in the way that something *flailing* moves or waves around.
2. *extra-*, "beyond"; *vagari*, "wander"
3. An *abode* is a place to stay or live—a home. That which *abides* is something you know will always be there, just as your home is a place you can return to.
4. Animals in a *pit* are *pitted* against one another.
5. The prefix *im-* means "not"; *placare* means "to please or appease"; *-able* means "capable of."

Using Words Correctly
1. C
2. C
3. I; People who are implacable do not change easily or often.

If Decency Doesn't, Law Should Make Us Samaritans • Good Samaritans U.S.A. Are Afraid to Act, page 23

Connotations
(Responses will vary. Students should give examples from their reading or personal experiences to support their choice of each word's connotation. Sample responses follow.)
1. N; *Allegations* are made without proof and have the effect of accusing people of something.
2. N; The denotation for *depraved*, "immoral," is negative, and so is the connotation.
3. N; Because damage or loss is involved, the connotation of *liability* is negative.
4. N; I think *rationalizations* are a way of avoiding the truth.
5. P; *Solidarity* suggests loyalty and resolution.
6. N; One who acts in a *callous* way is mean.
7. N; *Feigning* is trying to fool someone, to trick a person into doing something for you.
8. P; *Immunity* is like protection—a good thing.
9. O; To *construe* something is to interpret it.
10. P; Virginia's law protects, or *indemnifies*, people who try to help others.

Cumulative Vocabulary Review, Collections 1–4, page 24

Sentence Completion
(Answers will vary. Sample answers follow.)
1. Luis was *resolute* in his effort to find the hubcap for Naomi.
2. The *denizens* of juvenile hall were kids like Luis who had been caught breaking the law.
3. Someone who *dismantled* a computer printer would have taken it apart piece by piece.
4. Sheila Mant had a *pensive* look when she was lying on the diving board dreaming about a college romance.
5. Dating Sheila Mant filled the narrator with *apprehension* because he'd caught a fish, and he learned that she thought fishing was stupid.
6. Because of the size of the *concussion*, the fisher knew that the bass was a big one.
7. The narrator of "The Bass, the River, and Sheila Mant" expressed *resignation* when Sheila told him she was going home in Eric Caswell's Corvette.
8. To express *filial* devotion, a daughter might take care of her sick father.
9. The mudslide in Colombia was of such *magnitude* that tens of thousands of people were killed.
10. Rolf Carlé showed *tenacity* in trying to rescue Azucena from the mud.

58 Vocabulary Development

11. *Extricating* Azucena from the mud was impossible because her feet were trapped.
12. Viewers looked *stricken* when they saw the images of the dead bodies.
13. *Pandemonium* might occur if there was an earthquake in a large city.
14. *Presentiments* might cause a person to tell others about his or her fear.
15. It would be appropriate to *commiserate* with someone when the person has lost a loved one.
16. You might be *pitted* against nature if you tried to climb a tall mountain without experience.
17. A person who is *flailing* is waving his or her arms wildly.
18. *Rationalizations* for not helping someone in trouble might include fear of getting involved and being too busy to stop.
19. If you heard *allegations* of cheating, you would think that someone was making a statement without proof.
20. To show social *solidarity*, people in the United States might be more willing to help each other when they're in trouble.

Matching Synonyms

1. j   6. e
2. f   7. b
3. h   8. c
4. a   9. g
5. d   10. i

Collection 5   Irony and Ambiguity • Generating Research Questions and Evaluating Sources

Lamb to the Slaughter, page 26

Using Words Correctly

1. C
2. I; Barking dogs, shouting children, and arriving guests do not add up to a tranquil, or calm, day.
3. I; One would not take great pleasure in a loss one's team suffered.
4. C
5. I; *Premises* refers to a house and its surrounding property; the word intended here was *promises*.
6. I; One would congratulate someone on a victory, not offer comfort.
7. C

R.M.S. Titanic, page 27

Analogies

(Responses will vary. Sample responses follow.)

1. unconcerned (synonym)
2. happy (synonym)
3. unrelated (synonym)
4. diver, gymnast (related action)
5. unsuccessfully (synonym)
6. denied (antonym)
7. deliberate (antonym)
8. work (synonym)
9. chef (related action)
10. learn (synonym)

from *Into Thin Air*, page 28

Analogies

(Responses will vary, but relationships should not. Some examples follow.)

1. antonym; add
2. description; remark
3. antonym; dishonest
4. synonym; talk
5. synonym; industrious
6. description; decision
7. antonym; harmful
8. synonym; cross
9. antonym; shout
10. description; grasp

Explorers Say There's Still Lots to Look For, page 29

Related Meanings

1. b   3. d   5. d
2. c   4. d

Sentence Writing

(Responses will vary. Sample responses follow.)

1. It is an *illusion* that all corners of the earth have been explored.
2. Shackleton had been *marooned* for months on an ice floe.
3. On her spacewalk, Kathryn Sullivan *nudged* her spacecraft out of the way to get a better view of earth.
4. Sometimes explorers can feel a sense of *whimsy* about the amazing things they do.
5. On some expeditions the special job of *navigator* is required.

Vocabulary Development 59

Notes from a Bottle, page 30

Word Maps
(Responses will vary. Sample responses follow.)
1. *Connotation*: positive
   Synonym: movable
   Antonym: stationary
   Definition: able to be carried
   Sentence: We can bring the portable radio wherever we go.
2. *Connotation*: neutral
   Synonym: supposedly
   Antonym: unlikely
   Definition: probably
   Sentence: Presumably the rain will change to snow now that the temperature has dropped.
3. *Connotation*: neutral/negative
   Synonym: conjecture
   Antonym: fact
   Definition: thought; guesswork
   Sentence: Nothing definitive has been said, only speculation.
4. *Connotation*: neutral
   Synonym: plunged
   Antonym: exposed
   Definition: covered with water
   Sentence: The child submerged the plastic whale in the pool.
5. *Connotation*: neutral
   Synonym: withdraw
   Antonym: advance
   Definition: move back or away
   Sentence: We watched the waves recede from the shore.

Cumulative Vocabulary Review, Collections 1–5, page 31

Sentence Completion
1. On the *placid* lake it was still enough to read a book.
2. Mary Maloney loved to *luxuriate* in the presence of her husband, whom she dearly loved.
3. The blow to Patrick Maloney was *administered* with a heavy, blunt instrument of some kind.
4. The *superlative* qualities of the *Titanic* clearly outclassed those of all other sailing vessels.
5. *Titanic* crew members went below to *ascertain* the damage after the ship struck an iceberg.
6. To arrive at the *apex* means to "reach the top."
7. Sometimes rescuing injured climbers may *jeopardize* the safety of the entire expedition.
8. *Marooned* for months, he was forced to subsist on native plants and water.
9. The *navigator* is depended upon for plotting the course of an expedition.
10. The *clamoring* crowd made so much noise it was difficult to hear the speaker.
11. If the weather begins to *deteriorate*, climbers on Mount Everest must head back down for shelter.
12. Their *hospitality* was demonstrated by their allowing us to stay as long as we wished.
13. They *corroborated* the story by recounting the facts in the exact same way.
14. A *pertinent* fact is one that is important.
15. The *recriminations* began when the investigators assigned blame.
16. The *vintage* automobile was restored to its original condition.
17. Around the *premises* could be found various statues and other lawn ornaments.
18. The *garbled* message was unintelligible.
19. With a *quizzical* look I asked him to repeat what he had said.
20. In my *anxiety* I twirled my fingers and rocked back and forth on my heels.

Matching Synonyms
1. d
2. j
3. b
4. e
5. g
6. c
7. a
8. h
9. f
10. i

Collection 6 Symbolism and Allegory • Synthesizing Sources

Through the Tunnel, page 33

Using Word Parts to Build Meaning
(Responses will vary. Sample responses follow. Make sure that students grasp the meaning of each word as it is used in this selection.)
1. Sentence: Jerry felt contrition at the thought that he might have done something to upset his mother.
2. Meaning: *sup-* (under) + *plicare* (to fold) + *-ion* (act of): act of folding under, which indicates submissive or humble behavior
   Sentence: Because he cannot speak their language, Jerry tries to gain acceptance from the older boys through gestures of supplication.
3. Meaning: *defier* (to defy) + *-ant* (has): has defiance; is bold
   Sentence: The defiant opponent refused to admit defeat.
4. Meaning: *in-* (into) + *quaerere* (to seek) + *-ive* (quality of): quality of seeking into; questioning
   Sentence: Jerry's mother gives him an inquisitive look when she does not understand his persistent demand for goggles.

60 Vocabulary Development

5. Meaning: *minuere* (to lessen) + *-tus* (degree of): tiny; extremely small
   Sentence: Myriad minute fish swim in and out of tiny cracks in the rock.
6. Meaning: *in-* (not) + *credere* (to believe) + *-ous* (characterized by): characterized by not being able to believe
   Sentence: As the seconds ticked by, Jerry became incredulous at his newfound ability to hold his breath underwater.

Coming of Age Latino Style • Vision Quest • Crossing a Threshold to Adulthood, page 34

Related Meanings

1. d
2. d
3. d
4. c
5. c
6. b

Suffixes

1. Root Word and Definition: *gignere*, "to be born"; Part of Speech of Root Word: verb; Suffix and Definition: *-ous*, "having; full of"; Definition and Part of Speech of Vocabulary Word: "native"; adjective
2. Root Word and Definition: *solus*, "alone"; Part of Speech of Root Word: adjective; Suffix and Definition: *-ary*, "related to; connected with"; Definition and Part of Speech of Vocabulary Word: "without others"; adjective
3. Root Word and Definition: *dominus*, "master"; Part of Speech of Root Word: noun; Suffix and Definition: *-ant*, "has; shows; does"; Definition and Part of Speech of Vocabulary Word: "most frequent or noticeable"; adjective

The Masque of the Red Death, page 35

Making Meanings with Synonyms

(Responses will vary. Sample responses follow.)

1. *plentiful*; A plentiful stream of water poured freely from the spring.
2. *wise*; The king treasured the advice of his wise counselor.
3. *disease*; By taking the proper precautions, we can protect ourselves from the spread of disease.
4. *majestic*; The newlyweds spent the night in a majestic suite, the largest in the hotel.
5. *emerging*; A faint flicker of light was emerging from the crack below the door.
6. *quiet*; Those children who are quiet will be allowed an extra snack.
7. *spread*; A nervous laughter spread through the assembled crowd at the appearance of the stranger.
8. *ceasing*; A ceasing of activity occurred when the darkening clouds filled the sky.
9. *suitability*; The suitability of such a costume was questioned by the director.
10. *solid*; Although the form before us seemed like an apparition, it was, to our surprise, solid.

Cumulative Vocabulary Review, Collections 1–6, page 36

Sentence Completion

1. I felt *contrition* after realizing that I had done wrong.
2. A look of *supplication* means that you are making a humble appeal or request.
3. An *indigenous* coming-of-age tradition is one that is native to the country or area.
4. A *solitary* journey involves setting out alone.
5. A *vigil* is a watch kept during the normal hours of sleep.
6. With an *inquisitive* look he questioned me closely about where I had bought the ring.
7. Such a *formidable* presence is sure to scare off any intruders.
8. In a display of *ingenuity* he came up with a solution to the problem.
9. With an *implacable* stare she looked at us without blinking or relenting.
10. The young man *surreptitiously* spirited the candlesticks from the room.
11. The *luminous* glow filled the room with a soft light.
12. The *predominant* emotion at a wedding is one of tearful happiness.
13. The Red Death caused *profuse* bleeding that could not be stemmed.
14. The Prince thought to defy the *contagion* by sealing himself and his guests off in one of his well-protected abbeys.
15. The *cessation* of hostilities offered a chance for peace talks to commence.
16. Laughter *pervaded* the hall as the comedian continued her routine.
17. A *sagacious* person is one who is very wise.
18. The *notorious* criminal was wanted throughout the states of the Midwest.
19. I *nudged* the person next to me by softly elbowing him in the ribs.
20. The *crucial* decision settled the matter once and for all.

Matching Synonyms

1. i
2. b
3. a
4. g
5. h
6. f
7. c
8. j
9. e
10. d

Vocabulary Development **61**

Collection 8 Evaluating Style • Evaluating an Argument

Night Calls, page 38

Connotations

(Responses will vary. Students should give examples from their reading or personal experiences to support their choice of each word's connotation. Sample responses follow.)

1. O; The connotation of *inevitably* is neutral: It could be positive or negative depending on what it is that is inevitable.
2. P; To be *avid* about something is to be eager and excited about it, implying a positive experience.
3. O; *Indigenous* is a descriptive adjective that doesn't by itself convey a positive or negative meaning.
4. P; *Opulent* describes something rich and luxuriant, indicating, to most tastes, something positive.
5. O; *Adamant* by itself is neutral: It could be a positive or negative description depending on what one is adamant about.
6. O; *Abutting* simply describes the position of something in relation to another thing.
7. P; *Lauding* has a positive connotation because it indicates that something is being praised, and that is a positive assessment.
8. N; *Tremulous* has a negative connotation because it implies that one is nervous or scared.
9. O; *Patina* is simply a noun that names a color change that occurs due to age.

Call of the Wild—Save Us! page 39

Related Meanings

1. a
2. c
3. c
4. d
5. b
6. a
7. d
8. d
9. a
10. b

Sentence Writing

(Sentences will vary. Sample responses follow.)

1. Norman Myers argues that we destroy species by destroying their *habitats*, or the places where they live.
2. Few species disappear or are made *extinct* by hunting.
3. Some kinds of environmental *degradation* are reversible, but a species once eliminated can never be brought back.
4. There are both practical and *ethical* arguments for the protection of the environment.
5. *Consumerism*, or the buying and selling of goods and services, has had a negative effect on the environment when it has been excessive.

A Very Old Man with Enormous Wings, page 40

Antonyms

1. c
2. b
3. a
4. b
5. a
6. b
7. a
8. c
9. a
10. b
11. c
12. a

Cumulative Vocabulary Review, Collections 1–8, page 41

Sentence Completion

1. In "Night Calls" the *conservation* effort requires the keeping of the endangered heron at the Modder River sanctuary.
2. *Adamant*, the girl's aunt insisted that the girl be sent to boarding school.
3. The *tremulous* wail seemed to quiver in the evening air.
4. *Abutting* our yard were the neighbor's driveway and garage.
5. An *avid* reader is one who reads eagerly and excitedly.
6. If you are *lauding* a movie you saw, you are praising it.
7. Norman Myers argues that we destroy wildlife *habitats* through excessive development of the areas in which plants and animals live.
8. A species becomes *extinct* when it is no longer in existence.
9. An *impoverishment* of our ecosystem occurs when natural resources are destroyed or depleted.
10. A world *bereft* of wildlife is one in which much of what makes the world diverse and interesting is missing.
11. *Prudence* would dictate that you be careful as you move ahead with your plan.
12. It was *providential* that the rains came just when the crops were about to fail.
13. The *affliction* caused great misery among the population.
14. I *lament* that you lost your pet dog, a friend since childhood.
15. The young man's *impertinences* caused a great deal of resentment among those who were the targets of his insults.
16. It was quite *ingenuous* of you to believe everything that the salesperson claimed for the product.
17. Our progress was *impeded* by the barrier caused by the avalanche.

62 *Vocabulary Development*

18. It was easy to be *magnanimous* because we had more riches than we could spend in a lifetime.
19. The *opulent* costume dazzled us with its sparkling jewels and rich fabric.
20. A society obsessed by *consumerism* is one whose main interest is the buying and selling of goods.

Matching Synonyms

1. e
2. j
3. h
4. i
5. g
6. c
7. d
8. a
9. b
10. f

Collection 9 Biographical and Historical Approach • Using Primary and Secondary Sources

Where Have You Gone, Charming Billy? page 43

Synonyms and Antonyms

1. S
2. A
3. A
4. S

Writing Sentences

(Responses will vary. Sample responses follow.)
1. With *stealth* the platoon crept silently in the dark, disappearing into the shadows.
2. The night after Billy Boy's heart attack, the narrator's fears were *diffuse*, or unformed.
3. At times during their tour, the platoon *skirted* sleeping villages.
4. Soldiers undergo training to become *agile*.
5. The soldiers in the column seemed to be sleepwalking, pulled along by *inertia*.
6. Berlin imagines an ironic telegram that informs Billy Boy's father how *valiantly* his son had died.
7. When his foot had been blown off, the other soldiers told Billy in *consolation* that at least the war would now be over for him.

The War Escalates • *Dear Folks* • from *Declaration of Independence from the War in Vietnam*, page 44

Making Word Connections

(Responses will vary. Sample responses follow.)
1. facility; *Facility* means "ability to do something." Once one has the ability to do something, it is probably easy to do.
2. from the Old English word *gast*, or "ghost"; The *ghastly* scene brought terror to my heart.

Using Words Correctly

1. C
2. C
3. I; One wouldn't feel sympathy for someone whose team won a competition; one would be happy or congratulatory.
4. I; If someone can manipulate an audience, the audience will do what he or she wants.

The Sword in the Stone from *Le Morte d'Arthur*, page 45

Related Meanings

(Explanations may vary. Sample responses follow.)
1. d. avoided; *Confronted, challenged,* and *faced* all have the similar meaning of "stand up to; oppose." *Avoided* has the opposite meaning.
2. d. painting; *Painting* is a different kind of artistic technique than those described by the other three terms.
3. b. reward; *Promise, declaration,* and *oath* all have the similar meaning of "vow." A *reward* is "something given in return for a service or merit."
4. b. resolute; *Resolute* is an adjective meaning "determined." The other three terms are all related to the concept of social classes.
5. c. compassionate; *Tumultuous, spirited,* and *wild* all describe a certain type of excited behavior. While also describing a depth of feeling, *compassionate* means "showing sorrow or pity."
6. c. throne; *Throne* refers to the ceremonial chair a ruler sits upon; the other three words refer to the physical or geographic extent of a kingdom.
7. c. initiative; All the words except *initiative* refer to installing a monarch on the throne.

The Tale of Sir Launcelot du Lake from *Le Morte d'Arthur*, page 46

Etymologies

1. sovereign
2. diverted
3. wrath
4. oblige
5. champion
6. fidelity
7. adversary

(Responses may vary. Sample responses follow.)
1. A *sovereign* rules above or over his or her subjects.
2. If you are *diverted*, or amused, your attention can be thought to be turned aside for the time being.

Vocabulary Development **63**

Cumulative Vocabulary Review, Collections 1–9, page 47

Sentence Completion

1. Paul Berlin's *diffuse* fears weren't specific; they were unfocused.
2. The soldiers showed *consolation* when Billy became scared.
3. *Valiantly* the defenders of the fort fought against great odds.
4. By definition a *frivolous* request is trivial.
5. A *patina* of green appeared on the shell as it aged.
6. With great *reverence* I bowed down to show respect before the ancient shrine.
7. The animal's *terminal* illness would end in its death.
8. King argued for the *rehabilitation* of needy people in America.
9. King claimed that the world was *aghast* at the U.S. war effort in Vietnam.
10. King argued that the United States must take the *initiative* in bringing the war to an end.
11. The *predominant* mood of the crowd was exuberance, made evident by the rousing cheers.
12. With a bit of *whimsy*, I decided to play a little practical joke on the twins.
13. Was it an *illusion*, or did I really see what I thought I saw?
14. The congregation at St. Paul's, on leaving the church, was *confronted* by a stone thrust into a large marble block.
15. Under an *oath*, Sir Kay admitted that Arthur had given him the sword.
16. It was unheard of for someone of *ignoble* blood to be offered the crown.
17. At a *coronation* a ruler is formally proclaimed.
18. The knights of the Round Table *diverted* themselves with jousting and tournaments.
19. With *wrath* Sir Launcelot struck a tremendous blow on the helmet of his opponent.
20. When the waters began to *recede*, the stones of the riverbed, now exposed, glinted in the sunlight.

Matching Synonyms

1. f
2. a
3. j
4. i
5. b
6. c
7. d
8. e
9. g
10. h

Collection 10 Drama • Evaluating an Argument

The Brute, page 49

Synonyms and Antonyms

1. A
2. S
3. A
4. S
5. A
6. S
7. A

Using Words Correctly

1. I
2. I
3. C
4. I
5. I
6. C
7. I

Julius Caesar in an Absorbing Production, page 50

Making Meaning with Antonyms

(Responses will vary. Sample responses follow.)

1. *cheery;* The sunlit valley was cheery, in contrast to the gaunt surroundings of the dark forest.
2. *fatigue;* Far from vitality I felt great fatigue and could barely move a muscle.
3. *polite;* The polite waiter ran to get the chef, who by contrast was quite surly.
4. *conventional;* While the sister was unorthodox and would try anything new, the brother tended to be conventional.
5. *benign;* The benign smile hid an intent that was quite sinister.
6. *forward;* Don't be reticent: If you are not a bit forward, you won't gain the director's attention.
7. *certain;* His perplexed look slowly turned certain as the truth dawned on him.
8. *pragmatist;* Unlike an idealist, a pragmatist sometimes lets standards fall by the wayside.

Cumulative Vocabulary Review, Collections 1–10, page 51

Sentence Completion

1. Mrs. Popov pretended to be *indisposed* so as to avoid Smirnov.
2. Smirnov, claiming women to be *malicious*, asserts that he will no longer have anything to do with them.
3. Mrs. Popov felt Smirnov had dared to *insinuate* that she was all too willing to forget her late husband.
4. When Mrs. Popov is *incoherent*, she is rambling or disjointed.
5. Smirnov's *impudence* led Mrs. Popov to ask him to leave.
6. The *adamant* instructor insisted that we follow her directions.
7. An act of *emancipation* is one that sets someone or something free.
8. To act with *impunity* is to act without fear of punishment.
9. The *gaunt* stage on which Welles's production was mounted was grim and forbidding.
10. The *unorthodox* production was quite unusual.
11. Brutus can be seen as *perplexed*, or uncertain of his actions.
12. The *vitality* of the performance was thrilling and exciting.
13. The *surly* waiter threw the menus down on the table and stalked off.
14. A feeling of *inertia* made me keep moving without even thinking.
15. An *idealist* is guided by ideals, or standards of behavior.
16. The details of the *sinister* plan were chilling.
17. The *reticent* student sat in the last row and remained silent.
18. The *sovereign* ruled the kingdom justly.
19. The *relics* that were discovered probably had some kind of religious significance.
20. The grant of *immunity* meant that we were free from any legal obligation.

Matching Synonyms

1. c
2. f
3. g
4. a
5. h
6. j
7. b
8. d
9. i
10. e